7·52
ℵ
9/04

The Positive Woman

About the author:

Gael Lindenfield is a personal development trainer working with a wide range of organizations, from charities to multinational businesses. She trained and worked originally as a psychiatric social worker and psychotherapist, but as her career progressed she became increasingly interested in developing self-help techniques which can be effective in strengthening mental health and emotional well-being.

Gael initiated and led many pioneering projects for both the statutory and voluntary mental health organizations. Later, through her writing and work with the media, she succeeded in making her ideas and techniques available to millions of people throughout the world.

In her own personal life, Gael has also overcome many difficulties. She had a disturbed and often traumatic childhood, most of which was spent in a series of children's homes. In her adult life she has overcome many serious problems including recurring severe depressive illnesses, a divorce and the accidental death of one of her daughters, Laura, at the age of 19 years.

She now lives with her husband Stuart in Oxford. Further details on her work can be obtained from:

www.gael-lindenfield.com

Gael Lindenfield is author of *Assert Yourself, Confident Children, Emotional Confidence, Managing Anger, Managing Emotions at Work* (cassette tape only), *Positive Under Pressure* (co-authored with Dr Malcolm VandenBerg), *Self Esteem, Self Motivation, Success from Setbacks* and *Super Confidence.*

The
Positive
Woman

Simple Steps to
Optimism and Creativity

Gael Lindenfield

Thorsons

With much love and admiration, I dedicate this book to my daughter Susie who in 1992, when this book was first written, took her first steps into the world as a positive woman.

Thorsons
An Imprint of HarperCollins*Publishers*
77–85 Fulham Palace Road,
Hammersmith, London W6 8JB

Thorsons wesbite address is www.thorsons.com

First published by Thorsons 1992
This revised edition 2000

10 9 8 7

© Gael Lindenfield 1992, 2000

Gael Lindenfield asserts the moral right to
be identified as the author of this work

A catalogue record for this book
is available from the British Library

ISBN 0 00 710035 3

Printed and bound in Great Britain by
Martins The Printers Limited, Berwick upon Tweed

Contents

Acknowledgements

First and foremost, I would like to thank my husband Stuart who has given me so much emotional support and practical help throughout the writing of this book.

I would also like to thank the hundreds of clients, students and readers who have shared so openly their thoughts and feelings and who test out my ideas with courageous practice.

List of Exercises

Introduction

> No, I don't think I could write a book on positive thinking.
> GAEL LINDENFIELD, 1988

But here it is – and so yet another nail goes into the coffin of my negative demon! But I'm glad that I can still recall, and own, this initial response to a suggestion from my publisher. There are two reasons for this: firstly, it reminds me of the tremendous power which negative conditioning can exert on our minds; and secondly, it illustrates how important it is to have positive strategies with which consciously to fight such a destructive force!

As a therapist, I am probably more aware than most people of how negative thoughts, feelings and behaviour can seriously limit and damage our chances of both health and happiness. I have seen with my own eyes plenty of evidence to back up the research which is now proving the power of the mind's influence over the body, and I note that many people from other professions are also acknowledging this. For example:

- Even the most medically or surgically orientated doctors are listening to evidence which suggests that positive thinking bolsters the immune system and encourages the body's self-healing capacities.
- Cynical and sceptical die-hards of the business world are becoming convinced that a positively orientated work force thinks more creatively and has more energy than one which is depressed and fearful.
- Teachers are realizing that pupils learn more effectively when there is an emphasis on positive stimulation rather than destructive punishment.
- Coaches are fostering optimism and hope in their athletes, knowing that they can run faster, jump higher and shoot goals more accurately if they believe they can win.

So why should I initially have made such a negative response to my publisher's suggestion? The reasons were, I believe, both cultural and personal. The personal causes lie deep in my own personality structure. I emerged from childhood with major doubts about my own self-worth and the ability of the world to offer me any happiness or success. These doubts continued to be strengthened as I proceeded to disappoint myself with impossible challenges and cynical friends throughout my early adult years. Fortunately, one day as I reached the very depths of despair, I became aware that I had the choice of life or death, and that if I was to take the responsibility for living seriously I would have to take control of my personality. With not inconsiderable help, I taught myself to recognize my negative reactions, control them and replace them with a more 'healthy' positive approach.

The cultural reasons for my hesitance were mainly to do with my gender as a woman. At that time, the subject of positive thinking was most closely identified with the kind of success that is measured chiefly by bank balances. Its famous gurus were men preaching to ambitious work-orientated men; whereas I, being a typical female from the caring professions, had spent a career helping 'the underdogs' (mainly women) cope with much more mundane everyday personal problems with partners, parents, children, colleagues and friends. Now, just a few years later, men and women are moving much more freely between each others' traditional worlds. Many of my clients are now men – and I even run personal development courses in that hitherto 'alien' world of big business!

As a result of this cross-fertilization of ideas and experiences I am very aware that there are vast numbers of both men and women who are in need of strategies to keep them feeling and acting positively. In this day and age of multi-national commercial and government organizations, with the break-up of traditional family patterns and bitter philosophical, political and religious debate, who doesn't at times feel powerless and defeatist?

So Why Is This Book Addressed Specifically to Women?

Firstly, I think that women have a special need for positive strategies. For several decades we have been riding on the difficult but generally optimistic waves of the liberation and feminism movements. We now seem to be entering a new era. There is evidence of a backlash to our protests and progress. We can observe a current trend of looking back nostalgically at old values and wondering whether women 'have gone too far'. There is, for example, a revival of media and government interest in old-style family patterns, a cry for women to solve the unemployment problem by returning home to care for their 'neglected' children and elderly parents, disgust at American female soldiers who go to war with pictures of their babies on their hats, renewed interest in the anti-abortion and anti-contraception campaigns, and outspoken opposition towards women's ordination. We also hear that more women are resorting to drugs, prescribed or otherwise, becoming criminal, violent, suffering from heart attacks, becoming addicted to nicotine and alcohol, and risking unwanted pregnancy and Aids.

At the same time, in spite of the rise of 'New Man' images and ideas, we see many men and boys girding up their laddish loins. Others are using their insecurity and anger more constructively and getting together in groups to discuss new ways to respond to and live with the empowered women in their lives.

These kinds of backlash trends in the current times of severe economic and political stress mean that women's newly established rights and liberties may be in danger. So I believe that because of this situation and our long history of putting others before ourselves, we need the help and support that positive thinking and action strategies can give us. Learning how to empower ourselves by making the most effective use of our personal potential is vitally important if we wish to continue to assert our rights and find ways of capitalizing on the more optimistic social trends. We can take heart from noticing, for example, that green and peace issues are being routinely debated in the political world, and that there is a noticeable move towards a more caring, facilitative and participative management style in many major organizations. It is to our advantage that these trends are in line with feminine values and skills.

The second reason for addressing this book to women is that I am one myself! Accordingly, I have often had firsthand experience of learning to cope with the kind of internal and external problems which are discussed in this book. Because of conditioning, men and women do see themselves and the world differently; our interest and concerns may often be the same, but we may have differing priorities and even use different language to discuss them. You may notice, for example, that this book gives more attention to feelings and personal life than do most of the positive thinking books written by men.

Paradoxically, it was my work with men which made me 'super-conscious' of these differences. Several years ago, I found that, in order to be able to help men more effectively in my work, I had to school myself in the culture of masculinity. I did so for several years by taking an advanced academic course, and doing many research projects which involved talking to men about masculinity. But I know that this extra understanding and knowledge will never be completely adequate, and there always comes a point in my work with men when we become aware of their need to talk and work with other men. So, in turn, as a woman, I hope to be able to help other women more effectively.

How to Read and Use This Book

I have designed this book as a self-help course which can either be used by individuals working on their own or as a basis for group work.

It aims to do the following:

- provide an easy-to-digest explanation of the relevant theory and philosophy of positive thinking approaches
- present exercises, checklists and guidelines to help you identify your problem areas and find ways to make your thinking, feeling and behaviour more positive
- support you in your self-help programme.

I have liberally scattered the text with encouraging and enlightening quotes from a wide range of people, some of whom are 'experts' and others who are merely sharing the wisdom of their personal experience.

I was keen to use as many quotes from women as I could, but unfortunately these are hard to come by, not necessarily because they are less relevant or witty, but simply because they have not been recorded in the same numbers as those by men. Knowing this reality, I started to make my own list and collected a considerable number from listening to women on the television and radio during the year before writing this book, but unfortunately my own recordings are probably now disintegrating at the bottom of a Spanish river where the car-thief who stole my notes most likely threw them!

To turn to the structure of the book itself:

- *Part 1: Laying the foundations* deals with ways in which you can provide yourself with a firm positive base by:

- expanding your self-knowledge and becoming more self-aware
- challenging and changing your negative thinking, feeling and behavioural habits.
- *Part 2: Getting equipped* looks at practical ways to prepare yourself for action by:
- improving your physical well-being
- finding an appropriate image
- acquiring additional helpful skills and knowledge.
- *Part 3: Getting into action* gives guidelines and exercises to help you put the theory and the 'new you' into practice through:
- re-vitalizing your personal relationships
- changing your lifestyle with better management.
- *Part 4: Practical support* introduces a number of additional ways to help and support you in your programme for change, including:
- positive action strategy
- relaxation, meditation and visualization exercises
- the use of affirmations and scripting
- a reading list for further help and advice.

How long it will take you to complete the book and the course will depend firstly on your motivation, secondly on the extent of your difficulty, and thirdly on the time you can make available to do the personal development work. I would suggest that even the keenest of the keen would be pushing themselves if they expected to see big changes in less than eight weeks. Many people using my other books report that they have taken a quick read of the text for initial encouragement and a basic understanding of the method and have then returned to the books again to work through them at a slower pace so that they could digest them more thoroughly and complete the exercises.

Although, in my experience, most people find this kind of personal development work engrossing and rewarding even in its early stages, there will be times when you will be tempted to give up on yourself. This is why it is important to go at the pace which suits you – too fast and you will exhaust yourself and too slow you will lose momentum. The beauty of using these self-help methods is that you are *in control* and there is not the competitive element found in many courses. Who is to know, or care, whether you are working through the programme as fast and furiously as Jane in Auckland, Paula in Toronto or Gillian in Birmingham? You are the chief trainer and therapist. You must set the goals, plan the action, assess the progress and arrange the rewards. This book is designed to stimulate and enrich your potential to help yourself by providing you with inspirational examples, enlightening theory and hundreds of down-to-earth, practical ideas. Use it to empower and encourage yourself to overcome and control the negative demon within you!

Introduction

to the

2000 Edition

How well I can remember the struggle I had during the conception of this book. It coincided with a very difficult and turbulent period in my own life. Not only had my own country, Britain, embarked on a terrifyingly dangerous war, my own personal life was also feeling like one long continuous battle.

Our family had just moved house from a friendly and spacious northern corner of England to a more competitive, over-crowded, reserved town in the south. We had arrived emotionally and financially bruised from being badly let down by an estate agent. We were also sad and lonely at leaving so many loved ones, including our 17-year-old daughter. The house felt cramped and cluttered and totally without soul. It was very hard to see even the slightest chink of light at the end of the tunnel, which we had just dug ourselves into. You can imagine how I struggled to summon up the motivation to write this particular book!

A decade on, so many major changes have taken place in my own life, and in the world in general, that this period of personal pain seems quite insignificant. But of course it wasn't. Becoming a Positive Woman is all about learning how to surmount exactly these kinds of 'ordinary' troughs in our lives! Sometimes I think it is easier to find the psychological strength and motivation during the major crises that life brings. The more difficult challenge is to be able to hold on to a positive outlook through periods of more commonplace pressures and the routine slog through everyday life.

Certainly, writing *The Positive Woman* helped to get me back on track. I also know from my postbag that the finished product did the same for many thousands of my readers. So I was very pleased to be given the opportunity of doing this new edition.

During the last 10 years (in the Western world at least), women have generally made such significant progress in many fields that it is not uncommon nowadays to hear ourselves referred to as the stronger sex. Many of us have now broken through those infamous 'glass ceilings' and have begun to take up positions of serious power in both the academic and business worlds. The technology revolution has recently levelled the playing field of opportunity even further. E-commerce and mobile communications are making it increasingly easier for women to combine a family life with a serious career. On the other hand, the women who now *choose* the role of housewife are somewhat less denigrated and pitied. They are increasingly respected for making their ethically-based, informed choice.

But at the same time as all this encouraging progress is taking place, statistics also reveal that the numbers of women feeling depressed and despondent appears to be increasing. More and more of us need either legal or illegal medications or drink to get through our days. Many have become disillusioned with the stress, competitiveness and lack of balance in 'the promised land'. Many more are feeling frustrated and despairing because their personal reality is that this 'liberated land' is still denied to them. Others are just plain worried about the world in general, which often appears to lunge from one serious crisis and major upheaval to another.

So if you happen to be one among the very many women who still find it hard to stay as consistently upbeat as you want to be, I hope you will be quickly re-inspired by this bright new updated edition of *The Positive Woman*.

ONE

Laying

the

Foundations

CHAPTER 1

Basic Philosophy

What Is It All About?

We all know women who think and act positively even when the cards seem well and truly stacked against them. The individual personalities of these women will vary enormously – some will be quietly spoken and others will be the life and soul of every occasion – but I believe that they, and others who habitually think, feel and act positively, are likely to share the following basic characteristics.

HALLMARKS OF POSITIVE THINKERS

Progressive
Optimistic
Sensible
Independent
Trusting
Industrious
Versatile
Encouraging

Progressive

Because they themselves are continually growing and developing and they are interested in helping others to do the same,
positive thinkers are not afraid of the future; indeed, they look
forward to it with enthusiasm and interest. They are not
always looking back over their shoulders at 'the good old days',
even though they may appreciate and be able to learn from
their own and their culture's history.

Optimistic

Because they approach problems and situations believing that
a good outcome may be possible, positive thinkers do not
easily give up hope, so they are able to persevere through difficult times and setbacks. They believe that taking an encouraging view of the situation can often bring about a favourable
outcome.

Sensible

Because they carefully assess situations and prepare themselves well for possible setbacks and disasters, positive thinkers
know the advantages of sound organization and management
strategies and do not just allow luck or fate to guide them
along. They are careful to ensure that the goals, although challenging, are realistic, so they are not continually setting themselves up for failure.

Independent

Because they are at ease with themselves, positive thinkers
enjoy their own company and are not continually dependent
on others to make them feel happy or secure. They are able to
have satisfying long-term intimate relationships because they
can control their dependency needs and can allow other
people to have their individuality. They can motivate and
organize themselves and are capable of being self-supporting.

They are not afraid to swim against the tide and take innovatory steps forward or make difficult decisions.

Trusting

Because they have a high degree of self-knowledge and sound values, positive thinkers are able to trust themselves. They do not feel continually disappointed or surprised by their own feelings and actions and are therefore able to make full use of their spontaneity and intuition. They enjoy meeting new faces and are able to put their trust in others because, unless there is proof to the contrary, they believe that most people are good and have enormous potential. This means that they are both willing to lead and be led.

Industrious

Because they have belief in themselves and their potential and are optimistic about outcomes, positive thinkers are well motivated and can work with enthusiasm and energy. They try to ensure that their work is meaningful and rewarding so that they tend to enjoy rather than resent it. As they are keen to be working in peak form most of the time, they ensure that they look after themselves both physically and mentally. They are keen to stretch the limits of their potential so they make certain that they use all the educational and training opportunities available to them.

Versatile

Because they are confident of their own 'core identity', positive thinkers are able to move easily in and out of many different roles and make full use of the various sides of their personality. They are able to be logical and rational but also very creative and resourceful. They do not easily get stuck in ruts or become obsessional or phobic, but are open to new ideas and a whole range of different experiences and viewpoints.

Because they do not feel threatened by others' success, positive thinkers are willing and able to enthuse and lead. Without standing on a pedestal, they are willing and able to share the secrets of both their personal and public achievements and therefore can be an inspiration and guide to others. People feel safe to take risks and make mistakes in their presence because they do not demand perfection and are open about their own limitations. They want to take active steps to make the world a fairer, safer and happier place for everyone and, because they look after themselves well, they have the energy to care for others and engage in reforming or revolutionary projects.

I am convinced that the above are not mere figments of my idealistic imagination! They are traits which I have observed in numerous people who are leading happy, satisfying and socially useful lives. Some of the most famous examples are quoted throughout this book, but there are many others who live quietly but contentedly and productively out of the limelight.

I also see many people striving to achieve these qualities but often finding themselves frustratingly blocked, in spite of their supreme effort and motivation. Some of the resistance comes from outside forces, but often it is internal. Many people are becoming increasingly aware that *their own negativity* is blocking their potential to be the kind of person they want to be.

Negative Thinking

The sad fact is that very many people find themselves:

- afraid to take risks, so they stay in the same boring, unrewarding job or damaging relationship
- unable to take responsibility and assert themselves so that their children, colleagues or boss walk all over them

- giving up on their appearance and health by letting their body 'go'; perhaps becoming overweight, drinking too much, wearing themselves out, not bothering to 'dress up' or face the hairdresser's
- becoming increasingly isolated and lonely, as their friendships deteriorate and no new ones are formed
- getting more rigid and obsessional in their thinking and losing touch with their creativity so they are passed over for promotion
- not bothering to vote, so they get the government they don't trust
- too busy, too worn out or too despairing to give time to 'good causes' so they begin to project their guilt outwards with 'aren't they awful' and 'isn't it terrible' ineffectual moans.

No-one can say exactly how many women are suffering in this way but, judging from my post bag and other contacts, the numbers in Britain alone must be in the millions. Some people, of course, only get the 'black phases' occasionally and can cope by just waiting until 'it passes', but many others find that their negativity gradually creeps up on them until it is in danger of dominating their general thinking and lifestyle. My guess is that therapists like myself only ever see the tip of the iceberg, because most women in this state, even if they were well informed, would feel too ashamed, lethargic, despairing, cynical or powerless to believe that there was a way out of their negativity.

THE ROOT CAUSES OF NEGATIVE THINKING

Since writing the first edition of this book there have been great advances in the field of genetic research. It is now emerging that a number of our personality characteristics have their roots in our unique genetic coding. You may be more likely to become a negative thinker if, for example, you have been programmed with a temperament which renders you to become more than averagely depressed, anxious or angry when you are under stress. Your auto-response to problems will mean that you have less chance of seeing the positive opportunities than someone who is naturally calm and unflappable in a crisis.

Similarly, if you have been coded to be an introvert and you find yourself living in an 'alien' world full of extroverts (some families and societies are like that!), you may well find it harder to stay optimistic about your chances of thriving, simply because you feel like a square peg in a round hole.

More recent research in the field of neuroscience is showing that our brains' habitual thinking patterns do continue to be formed and set long after we are born. The most energetic and fundamental activity in this area takes place in our childhood. This is why the way we are parented and educated can have such a powerful effect on our basic attitudes for the rest of our lives. This is particularly true when we are reacting to life quite spontaneously and emotionally, and not in conscious-thinking mode. At these times it is as though we are being 'driven' by an auto-pilot whose programming was set by nature and our early nurturing. So it is no wonder we often feel (and sometimes behave!) like a child when we are under pressure and have no time to think.

Of course, there are many factors in our lives as adults which can cause us to view ourselves and the world negatively. The experiences of being continually discriminated against, becoming seriously ill or handicapped, being economically deprived, tragically losing a loved one, being the victim of a robbery or traumatic sexual abuse can all have very powerful negative effects, but certainly we have a much better chance of recovering our strength and hope if our basic attitudes to ourselves and life are positive.

> I was a first child, wanted and loved ... I am fortunate in that I am not a person of depressive temperament. When you become disabled I think it accentuates whatever your personality is. If you are of a depressive nature, you may become more depressed.
> SUE MASHAM

Is Change Possible?

> To improve is to change; to be perfect
> is to change often.
> WINSTON CHURCHILL

I know change is possible because, as I have already indicated, I have experienced it first hand myself, and have been witness to very many 'transformations' in other people. Although I know that, at heart, I was the same person 25 years ago as I am now, my 'personality' appears and feels radically different. I may not have become the model of positive perfection I outlined earlier, but I do now genuinely like myself, feel I have vast reserves of untapped potential to help myself and others, enjoy and respect the vast majority of people I meet, appreciate the beauty of the world and am capable of responding positively to its many challenges. This is a very different picture from the bitter cynical young woman who bungled several suicide attempts when the mood-lifting pills, alcohol and various 'princes' let her down!

My negative attitudes had been, in part, formed by early childhood experiences with an erratic, alcoholic mother, inadequate attention from under-resourced children's homes, confusing care and teaching from 'two-faced' nuns, and bullying from other equally deprived and insecure kids. But many other women have had a much more traumatic and unfair start in life than my own, and have managed similar 'transformations'. The great writer Maya Angelou is one:

> I decided many years ago to invent myself. I had obviously been invented by someone
> else - by a whole society - and I didn't like their invention.

There are various ways of overcoming negativity. Some people find their work, art or religion useful; others are 'rescued' by very inspiring and enabling people whom they happen to meet at some stage in their lives. The course outlined in the rest of the book introduces another way, which has been tried and tested by large numbers of people who have attended personal development courses or sought help from a counsellor or therapist.

I love the following quote from Catherine Cookson who spent half of her adult life being a negative thinker. She suffered a severe depressive breakdown before becoming a best-selling novelist and finding her way to becoming a positive woman.

> The word 'impossible' is black. 'I can'
> is like a flame of gold.
> CATHERINE COOKSON

CHAPTER 2

Becoming Positive in the Quest for Self-knowledge

> Knowing others is wisdom. Knowing yourself is superior wisdom.
>
> LAO TZU

Self-knowledge is a key factor in any programme of personal development. I am always amazed at how little people do assess their own personality and abilities. Gossiping amateur psychologists who speculate with great accuracy about the foibles or strengths of friends and neighbours often turn to the daily horoscopes for guidance on their own psyches! I have seen successful managers who have spent a whole career interviewing and assessing staff almost rendered speechless when confronted with questions about their own personalities and value systems.

Fortunately, however, there seems to be a change in the air – articles in women's magazines and newspapers are increasingly accompanied by searching questionnaires asking 'Do you always feel/think ...?' or 'Are you the kind of person who ...?' Of course many of these quizzes are written by journalists rather than professional psychologists or therapists, and give very superficial results, but they do nevertheless often start us thinking and talking. Similarly, in the worlds of work and education a fashion for self-assessment is sweeping through, as employers and teachers ask, 'What do *you* think you can achieve?' and 'What *personal* qualities can you offer?'

The penny is dropping even in the biggest of boardrooms. Recently I was standing in a queue at one of the leading management college restaurants and indulging in my irrepressible habit of eavesdropping. I was fascinated to overhear two executives from a major multi-national company talking about how they select staff at interviews. 'One of the factors I look out for is how accurate their self-concept is.' 'You're so right' said his companion. 'So many of the ones I see are way off the mark in this respect.'

But in our culture it is still not that easy to point the probing finger inwards.

We often have to contend with several negative blocks before we can confidently and enthusiastically take the path to our own psychological enlightenment.

Negative Blocks

Here are a few negative messages I have noticed ringing in people's ears.

Block 1: 'I don't want to be seen as self-centred or to look as though there is something wrong with me.'

It is true that there still is a certain stigma attached to self-evaluation. Contemplating the navels of *others* is now socially acceptable behaviour – in fact, it could be argued that it is even becoming quite fashionable. But to turn the same enquiring mind inwards still tends to be regarded as self-indulgent or neurotic. This is why most people's visits to personal development courses are initially shrouded in secrecy – who wants to be seen indulging in the pastime of the mentally infirm and selfish egocentrics?! But fortunately, as time progresses, more often than not I witness people who once came and went by the back door moving to the position of recruiting officer at the front!

Block 2: 'It's all right for those who can afford the luxury.'

I find that many people still think that this kind of activity is a privilege of the super-rich who have time and money to spare. Knowledge about affordable alternatives such as self-help groups, counselling and coaching is still far from common. Very often it is only gathered and given in times of severe crisis or when a problem has become so chronic that it is causing havoc in people's lives. The cry of so many of my clients is 'If only I had known years ago where to go to get help with understanding myself, I am sure I would not have got into this mess!'

Block 3: 'Deep down, I'm probably not a very nice person.'

Most people find the very thought of beginning to explore their innermost soul frightening. One worry which people have often confessed to me is that they are going to find out that they are not the person they hoped that they and others thought they were. They are afraid that a deeper analysis of their thoughts, feelings and potential will reveal their inadequacies, that the limitations to their 'niceness', intelligence and creativity will stare them in the face, and the reality of a mediocre or disastrous destiny will dull their dreams. This is particularly true of course for women, who have so many stereotypical images and archetypes of 'nice, caring back-seat drivers' with which to contend!

Every one of us has a darker side to our personality, however, and we all have limits to our potential. But getting better acquainted with our own 'devil' means we can have more control over her, and confronting the limits of our potential means we are more likely to set goals for ourselves which bring satisfaction and reward as opposed to disappointment and failure.

> I can't imagine anything worse than being a good girl.
>
> CHER

Block 4: 'If I start crying, I won't be able to stop.'

This is a very common fear, i.e. that 'digging up the dirt' through self-examination and exploration of the past experiences will bring overwhelming despair and depression. Certainly many people I have worked with find they have a very large backlog of tears to shed and do cry out at times, 'Will it ever stop?' But of course, it does, and then comes the feeling of relief and renewed energy.

As people become more experienced at doing personal development work, they learn to have more and more control over the buried tears and are able to choose to shed them in safe and supportive places – for example in the comfort and warmth of their own homes or in the arms of close and trusted friends who will not panic in the presence of their grief but simply be with them until it passes. As someone who has experienced the deep despair of serious life-threatening depression, I know that it is a condition of *non-feeling*, totally different from the reflective sadness and grief that we can experience as we recall and examine aspects of our past.

If any of these negative messages have been ringing bells for you – or, indeed, if you have any others – you must deal with your resistance first. If you begin your self-exploration with such attitudes, you will not only make the whole process feel like hard work, but you may also influence your objectivity, for if you expect to find trouble, your perception and memory will surely bring it out for you! Of course, you may recall sad times and experiences, *temporary* attacks of anxiety, self-doubt and cynicism, but remember that *that is not the whole story!*

> I knew that my cure would never be complete unless I could openly associate myself with two words; two words that had been my secret shame for so long, namely 'illegitimate' and 'bastard'.
>
> CATHERINE COOKSON, talking about her breakdown

14

EXERCISE: HOW NEGATIVE AM I?

Tick the response which is nearest to your own reactions in these 'everyday' situations.

1. When I get up in the morning, most days:
    a) I feel excited about the day ahead.
    b) I don't feel anything in particular.
    c) I have a feeling of dread or anxiety.

2. When it comes to planning a holiday:
    a) I feel excited and interested.
    b) I don't mind if others make the arrangements.
    c) I wonder whether it's worth all the trouble.

3. I think television these days ...
    a) nearly always has something interesting/amusing/ relaxing to watch.
    b) is OK to watch if you have nothing better to do.
    c) is just full of depressing news and badly made programmes.

4. A friend from long ago is trying to contact you:
    a) You're longing to tell her all about your life today and find out about hers.
    b) You don't think either of you will have changed but it could be pleasant to talk over 'the old days'.
    c) You wonder why she is bothering because you're unlikely to have anything in common, and anyway you are very busy.

5. You are about to go shopping for a new dress:
    a) You are excited and wonder what new styles are around.
    b) Your mind becomes immediately preoccupied with practical issues such as time factors, parking, which shops you should confine yourself to, etc.
    c) You worry that you'll never find anything you like or that most won't fit and that you'll either return

home without a dress or with one you have been 'conned' into buying – or, perhaps, that the dress won't really cheer you up in the way that you hope.

6. *You are glancing through the job advertisements in the paper:*
   a) *You notice all sorts of interesting positions which start you thinking about possibilities.*
   b) *You think that the situation is much the same as it ever was; you're better off staying where you are.*
   c) *You think that there is no point in applying because the job's either bound to be 'spoken for' or you wouldn't stand a chance against all those people who are better qualified/more pushy/older/ younger/prettier.*

7. *You unexpectedly catch sight of yourself in a shop window:*
   a) *You are pleased and satisfied with the image you see.*
   b) *You think (yet again), 'I must do something about my hair and get around to buying a new coat – and learn to stick to my diet ...'*
   c) *You quickly avert your eyes, wishing you hadn't seen what was reflected there.*

8. *You are on your way to collect the morning's post:*
   a) *You wonder who will have replied to your letters or if there will be any surprises.*
   b) *You doubt there'll be anything in the pile for you.*
   c) *You warn yourself that it's bound to be all junk mail and bills.*

9. *It's your birthday next week:*
   a) *You can't believe you're that age because you feel so much younger – you wonder how you can best celebrate it.*
   b) *You don't really want a fuss made of it, perhaps because you are too busy or would prefer to forget time passing.*

      c) *You know that you are likely to get presents that you don't want and receive cards from people that are only 'doing their duty' by you – the only good thing is it's an excuse for 'getting plastered'.*

10. *You are given short change in a shop; you complain and the assistant apologizes profusely:*

      a) *You accept the apology, thinking it was most likely to have been a mistake, but will remember to count your change carefully in future.*

      b) *You feel very sorry for the assistant; you seem to have upset her so much that you wished you hadn't bothered, and anyway what will people think of you, making a fuss over small change.*

      c) *You accept the apology very reluctantly; inwardly convinced that it was no accident because they are all 'at it' these days' ...*

11. *You hear there are plans to build a road through the children's park and the local sports centre:*

      a) *You decide to find out more about the plans and join or start an action group to ensure the residents' rights are protected.*

      b) *You are upset but suppose they must have looked at all the alternatives and just hope that someone makes sure they replace the facilities.*

      c) *You have a good moan about how planners are all the same – either thick or easily bribed. You know there's certainly no point in trying to fight 'that lot' – and the politicians are only out for the votes anyway!*

High scores in category:

'a' indicates a positive, flexible and energetic outlook. You enjoy life, and value both yourself and your time. You like challenge and are ready and willing to look at ways of changing your life. You know how to reward yourself and have fun.

You see the world as full of interesting possibilities and are able to enjoy meeting and relating to different kinds of people.

'b' indicates that you are in a lethargic, bored frame of mind and run the risk of slipping into negativity. Your life is proba-bly stuck in a safe, even peaceful, rut but there is a danger that you will one day realize that life is passing you by! You are too eager to please and probably the kind of person whom every-one likes but few would get passionate about. You are in danger of ending up in the classic female martyr position – wondering why people are not grateful for all that you have done for them and why life has let you down.

'c' – You have become depressed and cynical. You have lost your energy and enthusiasm for life. You see people as poten-tially exploitative, and are no longer able to trust. You have probably lost contact with your emotions. You may have resigned yourself to spending a lifetime 'getting by', licking emotional wounds and experiencing physical debilitation. You are in danger of forgetting what it is like to feel positive about anything and may end up feeling very lonely, even when sur-rounded by a crowd of warm friendly people. If you continue in this mode there is very little chance that you will be able to look back on your life with pride and a sense of achievement. In fact, you are in desperate need of some positive reprogram-ming and have everything to gain from giving the course in this book top priority!

Make a Positive Beginning

Start now to correct your negative outlook by reading the fol-lowing *typical* positive comments from people I have known who have taken the risk of inspecting the hidden depths of their hearts and minds.

'I didn't realize how exciting self-exploration could be.'

'I found out that I was a much more interesting person than I ever dreamed I was.'

'I'd forgotten how much I had already achieved in my life – remembering gave me the courage to keep on trying.'

'It was wonderful to rediscover my hidden strengths.'

'Finding out what was really important to me in life was the first step towards getting it!'

'It felt so good to become aware that I had simply slipped into a rut for the safety I once so desperately wanted but now no longer need.'

'Understanding the cause of my faults helped me like myself better – and helped me to become more tolerant of those weaknesses in other people.'

If you are suffering from a particularly bad attack of negativity, read the above section again and again. You could even photocopy it, paste it in your diary or hang it up in the kitchen to give you an extra-strong dose of corrective reconditioning! Now, with a positive, optimistic approach, try completing the following exercises.

EXERCISE: WHO AM I?

Answer the following questions. In the first instance respond quickly and spontaneously. Then, at a later time, review the exercise at a slower pace, noting whether you would want to change or modify your first responses and if so, why?

1. *The six adjectives which best describe me are …*
2. *When I was a young child I dreamed of …*
3. *When I was an adolescent I dreamed I would be an adult who …*

4. *The best that could happen to me would be ...*
5. *The worst that could happen to me would be ...*
6. *I feel at my best when ...*
7. *I feel at my worst when ...*
8. *The five greatest heroines I admire are ...*
9. *The five greatest heroes I admire are ...*
10. *My six great strengths are ...*
11. *My six great weaknesses are ...*
12. *I feel good when I think of ...*
13. *I feel bad when I think of ...*
14. *I feel hopeful when I am doing ...*
15. *I feel despairing when I am doing ...*
16. *I give of my best in situations where ...*
17. *I hold myself back when ...*
18. *I would end a personal relationship if ...*
19. *I would give up my job if ...*
20. *I would risk my life for ...*
21. *Most people think I am ...*
22. *When I die I would like to be remembered for ...*

Now ask yourself:

Who would I be prepared to show this to?
What might be their response?

> When one is a stranger to oneself,
> then one is estranged from others too.
> ANNE MORROW LINDBERG

CHAPTER 3

Healing
the Hurt

Emotional Wounds

> One must learn to care for oneself first, so that one can then dare care for someone else. That's what it takes to make the caged bird sing.
>
> MAYA ANGELOU

Once you have begun to get a clearer idea of the kind of person you are and where you want to go, you are ready to start the exciting process of reprogramming the auto-pilot of your unconscious mind so that it can help, not hinder, you to take your life in the positive direction you wish it to go. But before you can confidently glide along in top gear you must do some more preparatory work.

Without exception, every negative thinking person with whom I have ever worked has been suffering internally from what I shall call 'emotional wounds'. Whether these are new, acutely painful, bleeding hearts damaged by some recent trauma, or ancient festering sores generated by childhood distress, they usually need healing attention before the person can become truly motivated to adopt a more positive outlook.

So, if your self-analysis revealed a considerable amount of negativity, it is likely that you could do with treating yourself to a strong dose of loving nurturing. 'But how do I do that?' is a question that I hear many times. It is amazing how many women there are who are superbly skilled at nursing and caring for others but simply do not know how to turn these skills inwards towards themselves! No doubt you've heard people say, 'You've got to forget the past and get on with your life.' Perhaps you even tell yourself that daily! But, of course, it is easier said than done and *you* know only too well that you would if you could. You obviously don't enjoy feeling and behaving in a negative way, otherwise, I assume, you wouldn't be reading this book.

Most probably, along with other deprivations you may have experienced, you were never taught how to express sadness or anger efficiently and healthily. Perhaps you have been taught that you should:

- grin and bear it
- take the rough with the smooth
- remember that there is always someone worse off than yourself
- not cry over spilt milk
- let bygones be bygones

or perhaps you were not encouraged to express and share feelings of pleasure, excitement and pride. Were these the 'messages' you heard?

'You should never count your chickens until they are hatched.'
'If you laugh before breakfast, you'll cry before supper.'
'Little things please little minds.'
'Blessed is he who expects nothing, for he shall never be disappointed.'

Of course this kind of stoical, stiff-upper lip philosophy has its uses. In the *short term* it frees our energy to cope with the practical problems which most crises inevitably produce. It may have helped our parents and grandparents win wars and survive many dreadful tragedies, traumas and injustices which their rapidly changing and increasingly competitive world had no time to deal with effectively – and, of course, it helped our mothers and grandmothers swallow the bitter pills of the discrimination and oppression in their patriarchal world.

But what about the cost of using such survival strategies on a long-term basis to cope with the most minor day-to-day problems? We can see the answer all around us. This strategy has produced generations of women who are today weighed down with buried pain and the debilitating physical and emotional symptoms of stress, and many thousands of others who are merely kept afloat by their addiction to mood-lifting pills, alcoholic tipples, chocolate cakes or the fantasy tales of the soaps. Even women who have managed to find fulfilment and happiness can still harbour feelings of guilt, a sense of foreboding about the future and a cautiousness about tempting the hand of fate by simply being too happy and successful!

Modern research has now revealed that repressed feelings do not simply melt away – they are stored as emotional or physical tension, which can play havoc with our health and ability to live harmoniously and happily. But we can learn more effective ways of managing our feelings on a day-to-day basis and this is a subject we will be discussing in some depth in Chapter 5.

You can take an important preparatory step in that direction by confronting and dealing with that buried emotional tension which you are probably harbouring in body and mind right now.

EXERCISE: THE EMOTIONAL STORY OF MY LIFE

Using a large sheet of paper and some coloured pens, draw a series of pictures to illustrate typical scenes in your life which you remember with feeling. Don't attempt a great work of art; you can use symbols and 'pin-men'. Avoiding words will help you stimulate the creative and emotional centres in your brain and prevent you from making too many clever intellectual interpretations as you remember!

You have already spent some time reviewing your past history, but now is the time to dig just a little deeper into your personal 'feeling bank' and see whether there is any what we in the world of therapy call 'unfinished business'. By this we mean past situations which gave rise to:

- *feelings* which were never satisfactorily expressed, causing deep-seated tensions which may still be inhibiting the free flow of emotional energy and perhaps hindering you from being as spontaneous and passionate as you would like to be
- *thoughts* which were not correctly assessed and evaluated and may therefore have replaced your capacity for rationality and impartiality with dogmatic opinions and prejudices.

To assist you in the unearthing of your own 'unfinished business', complete the following exercise, which will help you review your emotional life to date. Remember that:

1. In looking for material we are not necessarily looking for 'the Truth', i.e. what *actually* happened, but merely your emotional reaction to *your perception* of what was going on. For example, your mother may not have been *actually* baring her teeth and threatening to kill you when you knocked down your brother's castle or came home late from the disco, but you may have *thought* she was and therefore felt the terror.

2.   We are not necessarily looking for major events or traumas. It is often in the everyday common experiences that most unfinished business lies. Indeed, the very ordinariness of the experiences may have resulted in their not getting the attention that they needed. We say to ourselves:
'Well, almost everybody has failed an exam in their life, haven't they?'
'All sisters quarrel with their brothers.'
'All my friends' Dads were just the same.'
'Every girl is terrified on her first date.'

It's up to you to decide in which order to look at your life events. Some people like working backwards, while others must always start at the beginning and others prefer working with whatever pops into their head – *vive la différence*! Just check out with yourself from time to time that sticking to your particular method is working in *your* best interests and is not just an old habit acquired from someone else with different kinds of aptitudes.

The examples I have given are merely guidelines rather than suggestions and should be used to help you structure your work. The next exercise can be completed over several days or weeks – but don't leave too long in between sessions or you will lose momentum.

EXERCISE: 'UNFINISHED BUSINESS'

Using your picture of your emotional history as a guide, try to summarize and highlight your own legacy of hurt from the past, noting how it may be affecting your feelings and thoughts or behaviour in the present. Try to be as specific as possible.

For example:

1.   *Mum's migraines just before holidays and any other exciting event left me with an expectation that there is a price to be paid for every pleasure.*

2. *Dad's inability to express any feeling except anger has left me wary and resentful of this emotion.*

3. *Mum's moans about having to work and the constant quarrels over who should do what at home left me cynical about the possibility of combining a career and motherhood.*

4. *My brother's bullying has left me with a fear of authority – especially if it is male.*

5. *My sister's gloating over her gleaming blond hair left me convinced that ugly ducklings like me are nicer people.*

6. *My family's general prudishness about sex has left me with a tendency towards frigidity.*

7. *Missing out on opportunities to make friends at school has meant that I have become too accepting of my loneliness.*

8. *The double standards of the nuns at school left me suspicious of all matters spiritual.*

9. *My dislike of the maths teacher has left me afraid to face figures.*

10. *My best friend's habit of flirting with the lads I fancied left me feeling that women can't be trusted if there are men around.*

11. *The extreme poverty of the neighbourhood in which I lived left me feeling guilty about indulging in any luxury.*

12. *My sheltered and over-protected childhood didn't prepare me for the real world.*

If you have completed this exercise, you may now be feeling 'churned up' and a bit depressed because you have probably reactivated some sad or perplexing memories. You may even have begun to feel a bit sorry for yourself – but believe it or not, that's good news! Of course, I certainly would not want anyone to remain in that position for very long, but to be there for a while can be very healing. I believe that it is vitally important that at some stage you must reach the point where you truly *feel* that, for whatever reason, you *did* have an unfair start or influences in life and that this has handicapped your ability to think and act in a positive way. I am not suggesting that you now become submerged in a sea of self-pity, but rather that, having recognized and acknowledged the injustice, you will be energized into righting the wrongs. You will be better motivated to give yourself a break, to beat destructive habits of self-blame and self-torture. So frequently I see these demonstrated by negative thinkers who depress and immobilize themselves with thoughts and comments such as:

'I'm a born loser.'
'That's just my luck!'
'Trust me to put my foot in it ... I've always had a big mouth.'
'I'm the jealous sort.'
'"Trouble" is my middle name.'

Emotional Healing

> When you start to love yourself, everybody wants to be around you because you have something very marvellous going on.
>
> SUSAN TAYLOR

On their own, the individual and personal experiences which you have highlighted in the last exercise may seem insignificant, but when they come in excessive doses they can turn even the happiest and most carefree children into depressives and cynics – unless they have been followed up by the kind of action which will encourage emotional healing. By this I mean action which allows:

– appropriate feelings to be discharged
– the experience to be assessed in some perspective.

When we are children it is up to our parents and parent figures to help us to heal. *Ideally*, when something happens which hurts or frightens us, whether it be a broken toy, a sick parent or a nasty nightmare – or indeed a more major trauma

– a caring adult will encourage us to *express our feelings* and, if necessary, hold us while we cry or shake with fear. If the emotion should be rage or anger, they will help us to discharge this in a safe and sensible place or channel it into constructive action. When the feelings have died down, they will sit quietly with us and *talk* about what happened -- helping us to understand the whys and wherefores, and accept the imperfections of the people concerned (even if these are themselves!), encouraging us (and showing us how) to put right what we can, or simply giving us 'tea and sympathy' to help us bear inescapable pain.

If we have been fortunate enough to receive this kind of help, as we grow older, we learn to take ourselves through this healing process or seek similar assistance from other people. We do not get stuck in the role of 'victim' – we get hurt but we are empowered to heal ourselves, pick up the pieces and move on in a positive direction. Moreover, we have the energy, skill and motivation to help others do the same, and we can gain much pleasure and satisfaction from being able to give such support.

The sad reality is that many people have not acquired this precious life-skill. Many parents can't, or won't, consistently help their children to heal emotionally from hurt. Sometimes they are simply too busy, too tired or too frightened. Perhaps they themselves have never been taught the skill. It is only a small minority, thank goodness, who are knowingly or intentionally neglectful. But whatever the reason or excuse, the result can still have a powerfully negative effect on the mind and behaviour of the adult who carries a collection of unhealed wounds inside.

In doing this self-development work, we are *not* concerned with blame, recrimination or revenge, but simply facing up to the reality of our inner pain and trying to do something positive about it. *We have to learn to give ourselves what we may have missed out on* – whether that be the time and space to feel repressed feelings, the opportunity to gather objective information to gain perspective on our experience, or simply comfort for our misfortunes.

So the next step I would suggest that you take is to give yourself a strong dose of *self-nurturing*. If I were your fairy-godmother I would probably whisk you away for a week to a peaceful and luxurious health farm -- but perhaps it is quite fortunate that I do not possess a magic wand because my idea of heaven might well be your idea of hell! But do you *know* what your idea of a week's self-nurturing might be? It's my experience that many people with a negative view of themselves and the world don't.

Positive people do know how to nurture themselves. They know how to give themselves treats when they are feeling blue or run-down and how to reward themselves if they have done well. Negative thinking people may sometimes seem to know how to do this but their 'treats' very often have a sting in the tail! For example:

- the big 'booze-up' which leaves you nauseous and depressed the next day
- the double portion of chocolate cake which leaves you feeling bloated and 1 kg heavier
- the trip to the cinema to see a horror film which haunts your dreams for weeks afterwards
- an action-packed holiday which leaves you exhausted and financially bankrupt
- an extravagant new dress which will hardly see the light of day with your kind of lifestyle.

So, when you are doing the next exercise check that you do not sabotage your chances of getting some *real* nurturing for yourself and certainly do not choose to do things which may masquerade as treats but are merely obsessional, conditioned responses to an addiction. For example: the cigarette to the nicotine addict, the whiskey to the alcoholic, the quiet evening in to the agoraphobic, or the afternoon in town to the shopaholic.

One of the common ways of sabotaging our chances of getting the nurturing we deserve and need is to depend too heavily on others to give it to us. As women, this often means *expecting* or *hoping* for a man to come up with the goodies – the well-timed cuddle, the listening ear, the box of chocolates or the surprise holiday in the Bahamas. Don't knock yourself for this bad habit because the Prince Charming myth has infiltrated even the most liberated female subconscious – just recognize your pattern and replace it with some self-nurturing action over which *you* have control.

EXERCISE: SELF-NURTURING

Make a list of activities which you know or believe could refresh you and help you to feel at peace with yourself and the world. For example:

- *a walk in the park*
- *a long hot bath*
- *an aromatherapy massage*
- *an evening at home watching a video*
- *a Mozart piano concerto*
- *a Julio Iglesias tape*
- *pottering in the garden*
- *some early nights with a good book*
- *etc.*

Make a list of treats which you already give yourself or could begin to give yourself as a reward for doing well or as encouragement when the going is tough. For example:

- *a trip to the cinema*
- *an Indian meal*
- *afternoon tea at ...*
- *a new book or tape*
- *a week-end away*

Draw up a healing action plan for yourself for the next four weeks, allowing at the very least half an hour a day to be devoted to one of the above activities or treats. If possible take at least one full day's holiday so that you can spend the entire time nurturing yourself.

If you have been very hurt and deprived by your past, you may need to consider doing an additional programme that stretches over many months if not years. Others may just need to do some short-term corrective work in certain areas, but I doubt if there is *anyone* who couldn't benefit from doing something. But remember, *don't set yourself up for failure* by giving yourself unrealistic tasks or goals.

> We cannot always control the events which hurt us or the people who disappoint us, but the resultant reservoirs of emotional baggage are entirely at our disposal!

CHAPTER 4

Kicking the Negative Thinking Habit

In this and the next two chapters, I will discuss ways in which you can alter your persistent negative habits in the three areas of thinking, feeling and habit. But firstly, let's look generally at the subject of breaking habits. The following are some guidelines I have drawn up which you can use to set 'programmes' for yourself if you want to do some serious habit kicking.

Guidelines for Changing Habits

1. **Check your motivation** – it is possible, but certainly not easy, to break most habits, so we certainly need to be able to see clearly the carrot at the end of the stick. We need to ask ourselves 'Who or what stands to gain if I crack this habit?'
    For example:
    If we ourselves are likely to be the beneficiaries:
    'Am I really worth all this effort?'
    'Do I love myself enough?'
    and if others will benefit:

'Do I love/like or approve of them enough?'
If an issue or cause is likely to gain from our efforts:
'Do I really feel this is worthwhile?'

2.   **Examine the habit** – sometimes we are so ashamed of our bad habits that we try to pretend that they don't exist. If someone brings up the subject, our guilt often stops us from having a rational, constructive discussion, and we just fob people off with 'I know, I know, I know, but I don't want to talk about it!' The result of this is that we don't give the habit too much thought until the big crises occur and we lose our friends, job, marriage, health, etc.

It is important to do a detailed analysis of the habit so that we can identify the precise *stimuli* which sets it off and become aware of what *positively reinforces* it (i.e. gives us a pay-off) and what *negatively reinforces* it (i.e. punishes us).

So we need to ask ourselves and others:
'When am I most likely to ...?'
'With whom do I most often ...?'
'In which places am I least likely to ...'
and the classic question for women –
'At what time of the month ...?!'

3.   **Set goals** – and make sure that these are realistic. We already know that negative thinking people regularly set themselves up for failure. They are hard taskmasters for themselves as well as for other people, demanding impossibly high standards and constant perfection. They often want to tackle the most difficult problems first and are not in favour of easy stages.

So we need to check that we are starting our programme with a task which has a strong chance of success and that we have a series of goals which will get progressively harder (but also progressively more rewarding) as we move on.

4.   **Practise** – if possible this should be done in a 'safe' place first, that is, in situations or with people where there is as little risk as possible to your relationships, finances, self-esteem, etc.

Two alternatives to practising in real life are role-play and guided fantasy (see Chapter 13). Other options might be preparing and reading scripts at home or using a tape recorder or video to give you feedback and practice.

5. **Monitor your progress** – you need to have some system for regularly checking how you are getting on. This could be entries into your diary, a wall-chart, or weekly discussions with friends or a self-help group. Whatever system you choose, make sure it is fool-proof against cheating!

6. **Reward yourself** – it may be a long time before you reach your desired carrot so you will need to find some way of encouraging and supporting yourself along the route. We now know that rewards are much more effective than punishments in any learning process.

Make sure that the rewards you give yourself at each stage are appropriate and that you save the big treats for the harder habits.

Overcoming Negative Thinking

> The quality of your thoughts determines the quality of your life.
> VERA PEIFFER

There are four steps which you can take to break your negative thinking habits and replace them with more positive patterns. These are:

1. Expose and confront your existing negative attitudes.
2. Adopt new positive approaches.
3. Expand your thinking powers.
4. Increase your exposure to positive thoughts.

Much negative thinking is essentially *irrational* – it is not based on well-considered facts and sound theories! It is directed by feeling and prejudice rather than logic and reason. Very often there can be *some* basis of truth in the arguments presented by this mode of thinking, but they rarely give the full picture. The process of censorship is often unconscious and is a habit ingrained over many years. We may be totally unaware of our discriminatory practices – although sometimes the 'madness' of our thinking may be blindingly obvious to others. We may hear:

'You're just being your usual pessimistic self.'
'Don't be so daft – how on earth can an intelligent woman
    like you talk like that?'

– but still remain convinced in our pessimism because we *feel* we are right, and so we defiantly defend our *opinion*. Yet our feelings and opinions are controlled by the parts of our personality which are not best equipped to make logical and rational decisions.

In my book *Super Confidence* I summarized some of Eric Berne's **Transactional Analysis** theory, which is still one of the simplest methods I know of for starting to understand more fully how your personality and its 'censorship' strategies work. As with many such theoreticians (including Freud!), Berne suggested that our personality has three fairly distinct sections and that each of these has a different approach to the world. In short, these are:

1.   the **Parent**, which is the part where our values and opinions lie; we use it when we are looking after, supporting, controlling, judging and taking responsibility for ourselves or others.
2.   the **Adult**, which is the part we use when we are being rational, objective and calculating.
3.   the **Child**, which is the part we use when we are being emotional, intuitive, creative, manipulative, rebellious, submissive, etc.

Each part has its uses and the secret of a healthy well-functioning personality is that each part is used *appropriately*. For example, we can use:

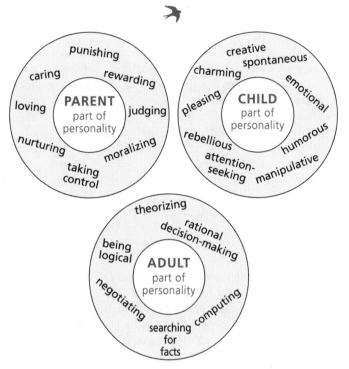

The Parent, the Adult and the Child

- the Parent to care for ourselves and others, make moral judgments and keep discipline
- the Adult to make important decisions and give considered advice
- the Child to have fun, feel the beat of the music or make passionate love.

But woe betide us if we quote too many statistics at parties, cry in a management meeting, or try to engage a mugger in rational discussion!

THE 'GEE' STRATEGY

Earlier, I noted that most negative thinking is heavily influenced by feeling and opinion, which are controlled by the Child and

Parent parts of our personality. These two parts have invaluable uses but we have to be particularly circumspect about using them if our childhood 'programming' was negative. You can override conditioned responses, however, by making a conscious choice to use the Adult side of your personality rather than the Child or Parent part. So I have devised a strategy whereby you can do just this. It uses your Adult to help you analyse your thinking errors. I have called it the 'GEE' strategy simply so that I could use mnemonics to aid the memorizing of the three habits which need to be challenged. These are:

Generalization Exaggeration Exclusion

Generalization

This is the habit of developing a 'no-hope' philosophy, based on a specific subjective experience. We had plenty of examples of these when we looked at the effect childhood can have on the development of our general attitude to life, but now let's look at the way many of us continue to reinforce these attitudes by continuing to think in a similar way as adults.

Specific Experience	General Attitude
A boy-friend who lied	→ Men can never be trusted
One full bus	→ Public transport is useless

Exaggeration

This is the habit of expecting things to be worse than they really are – worrying about a potential catastrophe before there is any real evidence to suggest that one is likely to occur.

Signal	Fearful Fantasy
A headache	→ A brain tumour
A late arrival	→ A fatal accident

Exclusion

This is the habit of ignoring the positive aspects of something and only seeing the problems and disadvantages.

Use the next exercise to check out your own habits and then try to use the GEE strategy on a regular basis to help you spot the irrationality of your thinking when you or anyone else spots negativity in your attitude.

Situation	Exclusively Negative Reaction
A new boss	→ 'I'll have to explain the problem all over again' (and not – 'A fresh approach to the problem might be the answer.')
A pregnancy	→ 'Hello, morning sickness, disturbed nights, big bills' (and not 'Hello, excitement, fun and love!')
Invitation to a party	→ 'Another late night' (and not 'I could meet someone really interesting there.')

EXERCISE: THE GEE STRATEGY

Over the next week note down any specific instances when you catch yourself thinking or reacting negatively. If possible, ask someone close to you to help you identify these habits, because more often than not we ourselves find it difficult to see the wood in our forest of problems!

Then use the GEE strategy to help you analyse your negative responses and see how irrational they are.

Positive Decision-making and Problem-solving

> In the long run we shape our lives and we shape ourselves. The process never ends until we die. And the choices we make are ultimately our own responsibility.
>
> ELEANOR ROOSEVELT

The next step is to replace your old habits with some new ones. You could, for example, just adopt a favourite habit of a former Prime Minister of Great Britain, John Major, who is reported to approach almost every problem by just drawing a line down the centre of a piece of paper and heading one column the 'Pros', and the other the 'Cons'. This simple idea is easy to remember and execute, and is certainly better than irrational negative thought. You may wish to try your hand at it and also at a couple of other techniques which I have found helpful.

FACE THE FACTS

This is a structure which I have devised to aid objective thinking when faced with a problem or a decision. It helps you to focus on five important aspects of the issue. Once again, I have used a mnemonic (For Against Choice Emotion) as an *aide-mémoire*.

1) FOR — the positive aspects: positive rewards, potential play offs.

2) AGAINST — the negative aspects: difficulties.
(Beware this section doesn't swamp the rest because you may find it the easiest to fill in!)

3) CHOICE — the alternatives, new ideas.
(Sometimes we are so absorbed in the stress of choosing between two options that we fail to see any others, including perhaps the option of doing nothing!)

4) EMOTION — the emotions which you and others feel about the issue.
(If you find yourself leaving this section blank, remember that there is *always* an emotional content to decisions and issues, and that if they are not obvious they are being repressed for some reason. Often this is because these feelings are negative, for example irritation, jealousy, cynicism or despair. Unless such emotions are honestly confronted and expressed they will affect your thinking in a hidden way.)

5) FACTS — statistics, costing, research data, time schedules.

> (Sometimes in the fear or excitement of making a decision or studying an issue we turn a 'blind eye' to the facts or omit to collect important data.)

If possible, don't try and tackle each of these aspects in order of sequence or at one marathon thinking session – you could restrict your creative thinking powers and your memory. Instead, put these headings on a sheet of paper or a blackboard for as long as you can before you make the decision or take any action, and then you can jot down your ideas and data as they come to you. In this way you may also gain more insight into your patterns of thinking.

At first you may find yourself filling up the AGAINST section, but as your basic mood and attitudes become more positive, the FOR section should start filling up.

Do the following exercise to give yourself some practice and then use it to help you to structure your thinking as formally as you can for a few months. After some time you may find yourself automatically thinking differently and you will not always need to go through this process – although I still find it an invaluable support when I am having to make major decisions.

EXERCISE: FACE THE FACTS

Think of a decision which you are trying to make at the present or one which you have recently made. Divide a sheet of paper into five sections as I have done below (or in any other creative way you can imagine!) and use the above strategy to explore the different issues and relevant facts and feelings. I have used the example of a decision to move house.

Decision: *Whether or not to take up the offer of a new job which would mean a major family move to the other end of the country.*

For	Against
Better career prospects	*Leaving much loved home*
Nearer to London	*Losing contacts*
Greater opportunities for children	*Initial cost*
More money in the long term	*Disruption of schooling*
Nearer the sea	*Countryside not as good*
Meeting new people	*Over-populated area*

Choice	Emotion
No change	*Excitement*
Continue looking for jobs	*Sadness*
Move in a couple of years	*Nostalgia*
Commuting	*Anxiety*

Facts
State of industry
Recession
Initial investment

How to Expand Your Thinking Powers

> There are hazards in everything one does but there are greater hazards in doing nothing.
>
> SHIRLEY WILLIAMS

Are you using your brain to its full capacity? The answer is most definitely that you are not – and neither am I! Research has revealed that most people use under 1 per cent of their brain. More recent research has shown that the brain can keep on developing throughout our lives, as long as we keep using it. This organ has quite staggering potential.

In recent years there has been much fascinating research into the differences between the brains of men and women. We now know that although we tend to have different areas of strength, both genders are capable of developing their weaker sides. (And don't we all know women who have become even better than men at the spatial-thinking tasks such as map-reading!)

In my own country of Great Britain, young girls are now in fact beating the boys in the academic world, but in many countries educational discrimination still prevails. Also, there may be many women who for personal reasons may have seriously underachieved. If you are one, take heart from the many inspiring stories of late-achieving women such as Catherine Cookson. I was also one myself.

So don't waste energy by looking over your shoulder and enviously admiring 'his incredible logic', 'her amazing memory', 'her brilliant imagination', 'his quick thinking', and so on – vow to start digging for your *own* latent thinking power!

MALE/FEMALE DIFFERENCES

Research has proved that the average man's overall IQ score is indistinguishable from that of the average woman. This may seem like cold comfort because the reality is that, although we have the innate potential to be on an intellectual par with women, very many women still do not have comparable *thinking skills*.

In the man's world that we were born into and reared in, women have indeed lagged intellectually behind men – because we have lacked the opportunity, motivation and inclination to develop and maintain our brains in top working order. Many of us were not encouraged to pursue higher forms of education, even though no one disputed the fact that we were as, or even more, able than the males around us. How many brain cells do you need to look sexy, wash nappies and bake bread? Until very recently it didn't make economic sense for the patriarchal society to educate us! Perhaps many of you, like myself, have experienced direct discrimination within the education system or from your parents. It may help if I tell some of my own story.

When I was 15 years old and in the middle of my 'O' level course, my family found themselves under severe economic strain. All four children were at private day schools to which my father had sent us two years earlier in an attempt to give us the best education he could possibly afford. I loved my school and was thriving both academically and socially. The liberal and encouraging atmosphere was helping to heal the wounds of a childhood mostly spent in repressive authoritarian children's homes. I was heartbroken when I was told that the family's economic difficulties meant that my sister and myself would have to leave our schools and join the state system. The pain of leaving my friends and having to attend a school which I knew would give me an inferior education was perhaps soothed by my sprouting social conscience, but I know the ignominy of having my educational interests placed behind those of my brothers damaged my self-esteem and directly contributed to my under-achievement at school. For years I put people with degrees (and clever people such as writers!) on giant pedestals. It was not until I reached my mid-thirties that I began to have a glimmer of my own thinking potential. I dread to think of the number of cells that must have died of starvation in my brain! The fact that I have heard many similar 'hard-luck' stories from women throughout my life has not assuaged the hurt, but it does fuel my determination to help women take positive steps to recoup their educational losses.

IMPROVING YOUR MEMORY

There are now many self-help books and tapes available which can show you how you can improve your memory. I have recommended a couple in the Further Reading section of this book. You have a vast store of information already in your brain which you probably hardly use. If you exercise your 'recall muscles', you will find yourself remembering things which you thought had been buried forever in the recesses of your mind. You can do this quite simply – by, for example:

keeping a daily diary.
learning a language.
learning some poems or quotes off by heart.

Psychologists have also shown that we can also improve our ability to *retain* information by:

- keeping our study periods short
- constantly reviewing what we have learned
- repeating information, such as a name, several times as soon as we hear it
- using mnemonic techniques which help us make links
- using highlighting colours
- using symbols, drawings and stories to illustrate the data we are trying to memorize
- making our learning into a fun game
- asking others to test us.

IMPROVING YOUR ABILITY TO LOOK AND LISTEN

Highly tuned observation and listening skills are essential to clear rational thinking. Our eyes and ears are incredibly adept at selecting out information according to the mood we are in – if we 'get out of the wrong side of the bed' we don't even look for the blue sky, or if we've been told to expect a boring speech, we'll sleep through the juicy bits!

Here are some ways in which you can take better control of these senses and encourage them to give you beneficial information:

- Practise your concentration by spending five minutes a day selecting and focusing on certain sounds such as bird song or a ticking clock, and consciously switching off other distracting sounds.
- Check that your body is in an alert position – no slouching or wandering eyes.
- Close your eyes occasionally and practise recalling in detail what you have just seen.
- If you find yourself 'switching off' from someone who is boring, put yourself into the role of constructive critic.
- Use the classic counselling technique of 'Reflection' to check out your listening skills, i.e. summarize what has

been said by repeating back to the speaker what they have said. If you use slightly different words you won't sound like a parrot!

– Use drawing regularly to observe detail (not to produce great works of art for public consumption!)

– In the privacy of your own home, practise the art of 'mimicking' various people, not to make fun of them but to improve your ability to observe their finer points. (This is a skill we were all born with – what young child can't mimic its parents with uncomfortable accuracy!)

– Take notes – but don't play stenographer, just jot down key words.

– Look after your ears and your eyes by not overloading them and giving them plenty of time to rest.

– Continually make a conscious effort to switch your body into a relaxed state, as physical tension impairs both sight and hearing.

IMPROVING YOUR READING AND NOTE-TAKING

Reading can have many uses – it can give information and offer relaxing distraction, but if used *in collaboration with thinking* it can stimulate imaginative and energizing thought.

When you picked up this book, did you open it at the beginning and begin dutifully reading each page in sequence? I hope not. Although I, as an author, have tried to work to some kind of order (and may *feel* quite protective of that order if my editor should start wanting to move bits and pieces around!), I do *know* that the way I have arranged information is not going to suit the needs of very many readers. So I would like to think that when you picked up this book, you did a quick flick through to see what bits were of interest to you *as an individual with particular needs* and that you then selected the chapters you wanted, and needed, to read. If you did this you may not, of course, actually need to read any more of this section because you have already developed a flexible approach to reading!

For those of you who *are* choosing to read on, here are some tips which have helped me and many of my clients:

- Vow to make reading a pleasure and don't tolerate boredom. Whenever possible skip the boring bits and give yourself full permission to change your mind. (I dread to think how many hours of my life I used to waste reading books to the bitter end just because I had started them!)
- To aid concentration, always check that you are sitting reasonably upright but comfortably.
- For speed-reading a text, use a pencil or similar marker to guide you along the lines. This technique is supposed to increase reading speed by as much as 100 per cent, because it focuses attention and improves concentration.
- Read the contents tables and the beginning and end of chapters before ploughing through a long text. Use the index to find particular sections of interest and go to those first.
- Keep your eyes working efficiently by regularly looking away, blinking or cupping your hands over them.
- Make notes in the margin, or on a card which can double as a book marker. At the end of each chapter, or after no more than 20 minutes, enter these notes to a Mind Map like the one illustrated in the next exercise. This will help you retain the information and save you rereading the whole book.
- When you have finished the book, file your references and ideas, using the heading from your Mind Map as a guide for your index. If you have been making notes on a card, use an alphabetical card index to file it under the author's name.

EXERCISE: MIND MAP NOTE-TAKING

Take notes in 'Mind Map form' from a chapter of this book.

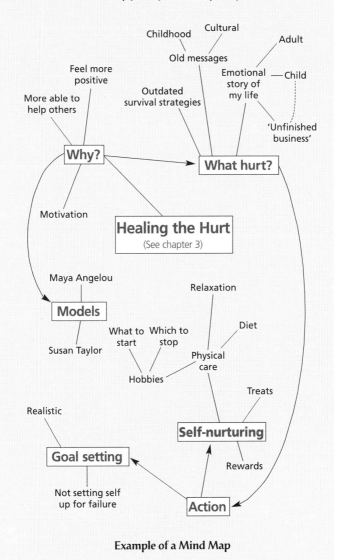

Example of a Mind Map

EXERCISE: BRAINSTORMING

Brainstorming is a 'creative' form of note-taking:

– Place an idea in the centre of the page.
*– Jot down any words or phrases which come into your head –
never censoring any which may at the time seem daft or
inappropriate.*
*– When ideas or thoughts have stopped flowing, you can begin to
make sense of the notes: weeding out the nonsense, expanding
on the useful, etc. Work until you establish some order in your
thoughts.*

Here is an example opposite.

Stage 1

success   decisive   standing tall
self-respect   Self-esteem   relaxed
giving criticism   taking criticism   eye contact
firm handshake   smart
self defence   **CONFIDENCE**
challenge   saying no   courage   reward   energetic
bullying   risks   not afraid   looking good   women in suits
not caring for others   getting own way   sales people   politicians

Stage 2

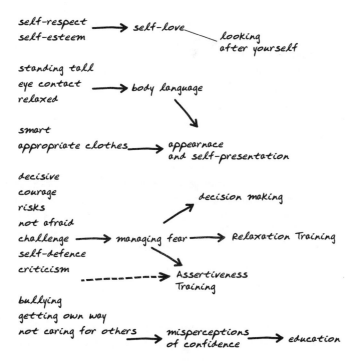

self-respect
self-esteem → self-love — looking after yourself

standing tall
eye contact → body language
relaxed

smart
appropriate clothes → appearnace and self-presentation

decisive
courage
risks
not afraid
challenge → managing fear → Relaxation Training
self-defence
criticism - - - - - → Assertiveness Training

bullying
getting own way
not caring for others → misperceptions of confidence → education

→ decision making

IMPROVING YOUR NUMERACY

My family find it very hard to believe that I achieved the top grade in my 'O' level maths because, like very many women, on leaving school I allowed my mathematical ability to languish in the darkest recesses of mind for very many years, until I reached a stage where I was barely able to count my change! Every so often I became resentful and irritated by my dependence on my husband's arithmetic agility, but it was self-induced. Now that I work on a freelance basis and am responsible for my own budgets and bookkeeping, I am having to resurrect my rusty mathematical potential so that I can be in control of my financial life.

Are you being held back by your lack of skills and knowledge in this area? If so, you can do something constructive to correct your under-achievement. I am assured, on the good authority of maths teachers and their mature female students, that studying this subject need not be boring or tedious. There are many new techniques, games and tricks which make learning both interesting and fun. As this is not my area of excellence, I have not included exercises in this section, but there are many self-help books on this subject and there are also courses at adult education centres. Take heart, as I and many other women have done, from some more of Tony Buzan's wisdom:

> In the past it was assumed that some people were basically capable in mathematics and others were not, no matter how much assistance they were given. What we now know, of course, is that the brain has almost limitless capacity, and that this ranges over all subjects ... any 'disability' that we may have is probably due to our leaving that area untended, rather than to any inherent fault in the working of the brain.

Improving your numeracy could also give your confidence a welcome boost because some interesting American research has revealed that young women with high mathematical ability have a significantly higher opinion of themselves and their

ability to control their own lives than their less numerate con-
temporaries.

IMPROVING YOUR CREATIVE POTENTIAL

Just as we have the potential to be more numerate we can all
become more creative if we choose to do so, and this is an area
where I *can* claim to have had some personal achievement! An
important milestone for me was finding out about research
into the functions of the left and right brain and then reading
further accounts of how people were using this knowledge to
increase their creativity and improve their thinking capacities.
As a result, I did many exercises and courses. These did not
reveal latent genius of the Mozartian or Van Goghian kind, but
I know that it did transform my problem-solving capacities by
reviving my flagging imagination, intuition and spontaneity.

The Left and Right Brain

The brain is divided into two sections. Although research in
this field is still developing, most neuroscientists agree that
each side has particular 'responsibility' for controlling the specific functions which I have illustrated below, and that most of
us have one side which is more dominant than the other. We
can dramatically increase our brain-power by stimulating our
lazy side, which can be achieved by doing certain activities.

Modern Western education has sorely neglected the development of right brain activity, only minimally stimulating it
for the limited production of works of art by a 'lucky' few.
Most of us have been more conditioned to think in a logical,
analytical and linear way. We have not been trained to see the
'jigsaw' as a whole, only the individual pieces. We tend to see a
series of symptoms and not the general patterns in a problem
situation and therefore we are not tackling root causes or
coming up with enough radically new ideas. In the field of
medicine, many people are thankfully beginning to see the
importance of viewing health in an holistic manner and to see
the value of right brain approaches and skills such as hypnosis,

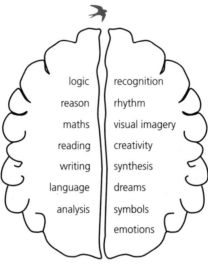

Left brain   Right brain

The left and right brain

creative visualization, art and drama therapy. But this kind of thinking can be useful in many other fields. It is becoming increasingly popular in progressive management training programmes, and is now widely used by counsellors and therapists engaged in helping people find solutions to personal problems.

> Imagination is more than knowledge.
> ALBERT EINSTEIN

Here are some self-help ideas for stimulating and exercising the right side of your brain – but don't forget that creativity, like left-brained analytical activities, requires discipline and pragmatism if it is to be harnessed and used constructively.

- **Learn deep-relaxation techniques** and use them to give yourself regular chances to daydream. Research into the personality and behaviour of original and creative story writers revealed that they spent frequent periods daydreaming.

- **Practise meditation.** I have found one of the easiest ways is to focus my attention on the central point of a drawing or painting designed in the form of a mandala. When focusing on the mandala, your left brain is out of action, because it is the right side that is used to make sense out of this kind of spatial information. I have had some mandalas specially painted in restful colours and often use them as a warm-up in my groups before we begin to use creative therapy techniques such as art or drama.

EXERCISE: MANDALA MEDITATION

Focus on the centre of one of the mandalas for five to ten minutes. When your eyes begin to wander, gently bring them back to the centre.

If possible, play some quiet rhythmic music.

Do this exercise for five minutes each day until you become skilled at it. Then do it at regular intervals, or before you want to activate your creativity in order to come up with some ideas. You can also use it when you want to give your left brain a rest – perhaps when it has 'gone fuzzy' with too much analysing!

- **Listen to more music** (but stop your left brain from working out the harmonies and imperfect cadences!)

- **Start doodling and drawing**, using symbols instead of words whenever you can. Join an art class.
- **Join in imaginative play** with children or do improvisation games with your friends. Find an adventurous drama group.
- **Make up stories** for your children rather than reading them books all the time. Begin to write short stories of your own.
- **Have fancy dress or theme parties** and be stimulated by other people's imagination and spontaneity.
- **Use role-play and games in staff training.**
- **Use Mind Map and Brainstorms** (see above) for making notes and stimulating discussion.
- **Listen to your dreams** – but don't rely on too many dream manuals. Exercise your own creativity and, whenever possible, make your own interpretations. The symbolism in dreams is usually very personal and I am convinced that most people are the best judges of their own metaphors. For example, for me the image of a wilderness is full of fear and foreboding, whereas for others it could be calming and restful.

  If you have a partner or friend who will listen without playing amateur psychologist, it can be stimulating to talk through your dreams with them. I look back with nostalgia to the time when my daughters were younger and we would start the day sharing tea and our dreams, cuddled up together in bed. It felt a very healing practice and I can fully believe that there may be some link between the peaceful nature of the Senoi tribe in Malaya and their practice of sharing dreams in a village community meeting each morning.

  Experimenting with being your own dream analyst will be good stimulation for your right brain and may give you some valuable insights. Some dreams are non-events, just recordings of the filing system of your unconscious at work. Others are undoubtedly trying to convey a message to your conscious self that there is some 'unfinished business' still lurking around. Maybe you have a relationship problem to sort out, a feeling that needs discharging or an inner conflict that needs resolving – if so, when you have done the exercise, don't forget to use the wisdom you have gained.

If self-help doesn't work or appeal to you, either consider joining a group where this could be explored, or find a therapist who has been professionally trained to work with dreams (e.g. Jungian analysts, art therapists, drama therapists and psychodramatists).

EXERCISE: INTERPRETING YOUR DREAMS

Find a place where you can be quiet and relaxed and talk yourself through the dream again, as though it were happening in the present.

If the dream felt unfinished, imagine an ending.

Take special note of the feelings and powerful images. Remembering that dream feelings often relate to those we are trying to deny, and that dream images are often metaphors for parts of ourselves, try to make some connection with the major issues and internal conflicts that are going on in your life.

Note down what action you are going to take, for example: 'I must make a decision about ...', 'I will talk to him about ...'

Exposing Yourself to Positive Thoughts

There is a common belief that opposites attract. In fact, the contrary is more often true. The majority of people consciously or unconsciously seek out mirror images of themselves because this helps them firm up their sense of identity and gives them a feeling of security. Ghettos of immigrants are an obvious example, but in ordinary everyday situations just think what a boost you feel when you meet someone with whom you 'just clicked' and how 'at home' you feel when in the company of 'like minds'.

So, if you are negatively inclined, it is highly likely that you will have fallen into the habit of surrounding yourself with friends and colleagues who are of similar ilk and are continually reinforcing your pessimism, cynicism, melancholy and despair. I have found that many of my clients' favourite artists and poets are people who had a history of severe depression. Virginia Woolf is a good example. Her books were often passed around psychiatric wards in which I used to work. She was, of course, a brilliant poet and novelist, and much of her work has been very inspiring to feminists, but I have seen many negative thinkers sink themselves even further into despair through 'overdosing' on her work.

Do you discuss gloomy statistics and potential disasters with your friends, compete over 'awful men' stories, gloat as you share 'I told you so' and 'I knew it would end in disaster' stories or simply drink, eat or work yourself to death? Often this kind of activity is deceptively packaged as fun or support!

Albert Ellis, an American psychologist who was the father of Rational Emotive Therapy (RET) suggested that Western culture itself was inculcated with many irrational ideas which he felt were responsible for much neurosis. He identified 11 of these which I have used to form the basis of the checklist in the following exercise.

EXERCISE: THE IRRATIONAL CULTURE

Read through the following list of 'beliefs', asking yourself whether these ideas and values are ones which, at least to some extent or on some occasions, inhabit your world. At first they may seem rather extreme and too general, but I have found that left in this form, they are more confrontational. Although they may not be made explicit, Albert Ellis suggests that they are embedded in the Western culture, therefore it is likely that their philosophy and morality could permeate the books or newspapers you read, the television programmes you watch, the church you attend or even the work that you do. Make notes of examples of these values and ideas during the next week. Show the list to friends and colleagues and start talking!

1. *It is essential that a person be loved or approved of by virtually everyone in the community.*
2. *A person must be perfectly competent, adequate and achieving to be considered worthwhile.*
3. *Some people are bad, wicked or villainous and therefore should be blamed and punished.*
4. *It is a terrible catastrophe when things are not as a person wants them to be.*
5. *Unhappiness is caused by outside circumstances, and a person has no control over it.*
6. *Dangerous or fearsome things are of great concern, and their possibility must be continually dwelt on.*
7. *It is easier to avoid certain difficulties and self-responsibilities than to face them.*
8. *A person should be dependent on others and should have someone stronger on whom to rely.*
9. *Past experiences and events are the determinants of present behaviour; the influence of the past cannot be eradicated.*
10. *A person should be quite upset over other people's problems and disturbances.*

Although I agree with Ellis that most of these ideas are very widespread, it is still possible to find alternatives! We have to take responsibility for feeding ourselves with ideas and experiences which are more rational and encouraging. I am certainly not suggesting that we should completely blinker ourselves to the pain and problems of living, but, as I suggested earlier, over-emphasis on difficulties feeds negative thinking, burnout and feelings of powerlessness. I often hear people say:

'There's *no point* in doing that because
 ... no marriage is ever really happy after the first two years.
 ... all jobs are boring when you get to know more about them.
 ... all people are selfish when they're put to the test.

... everything becomes dull if you do it long enough.
... there's never anything good on television.
... everything you read in newspapers is depressing.
... all comedians are cynics or depressives at heart.
... it will be out of date by the time I've learned it.
... women will always bitch behind your back.'

and I can fully empathize with them because this habit is one that took me many years to break and still has a tendency to return (as do most habits which have their roots in childhood) when I am under excessive stress or strain.

For the next few weeks, why not take some risks and break with many of your familiar niggly negative habits. Give yourself a chance to meet, either directly or indirectly, positive thinking people. I have given you some examples of how you could achieve this in the next exercise, but it will be much more successful if you set your own goals. These will help alter your overall mood and give you new ideas and information.

EXERCISE: POSITIVE EXPERIENCES

Make a list of things you can do in the next few weeks which will give you a 'lift' and help you to feel more positive.
  For example:

1. *Watch more comedy shows on television.*
2. *Book to see a musical or some other fun event.*
3. *Read an autobiography of some successful and happy person.*
4. *Insist on hearing the good news from friends.*
5. *Go for an early evening walk on the beach or in the park.*
6. *Ask a woman who is happily married what her life is like.*
7. *Ask relatives to tell you about the best times in their lives.*
8. *Start up a conversation with people on the train who look relaxed and happy.*
9. *Join an art appreciation class.*

Now that you have given yourself a substantial 'shot' of positive thoughts, try working out a new belief system for yourself. Start a collection of positive and encouraging proverbs or quotes, make posters of them and put them up at home or in the office.

Examples:

One day of pleasure is worth two of sorrow.
It's an ill wind that blows no good.
Fortune favours the brave.
Good words cost nought.
Knowledge is power.
Possibilities are infinite.
Many drops make a shower.
Union is strength.
Every oak has been an acorn.
Great hopes make great women.
When one door closes, another opens.

Next do the following exercise.

EXERCISE: CREDO

Positively complete the sentence 'I believe ...' as many times as you can.

Examples:

I believe that I am an exciting and unique person with loads of potential.
I believe that I can be assertive and powerful.
I believe that I can love and be loved.
I believe that I can have many good friends.
I believe that the environment can be preserved.
I believe that there are alternatives to war.
I believe that people can change for the better as well as for the worse.
I believe that I can be successful at work.

Then, having read and reread your Credo several times, pin it up in the office or kitchen - or anywhere where it will stare you in the face with annoying frequency!

The thoughts, attitudes and beliefs of a positive woman are her own, and she is proud to have them.

CHAPTER 5

Kicking
Negative
Habits of
Feeling

> 'Love is a compulsive, obsessive disorder'
> HEADLINE - *INDEPENDENT* 14.02.00

This headline caught my eye at breakfast this morning. The article claimed that psychologists say that 'neuro-chemistry of love can be a drug as difficult to give up as alcohol or cocaine.'

Even though you may dismiss this 'news' as a rather dubious offering from a journalist desperate to find a new angle for Valentine's Day, it does raise an important point. Many people (particularly women) do feel as controlled by their feelings as they would be by a physical substance to which they had become addicted. I am continually consulted by people who know that they are being held back from getting the life they want because they find themselves:

– paralysed and restricted by panic attacks which appear to come out of the blue
– overwhelmed by depression which they are unable to shake off

– frightened by their temper blowing up at inopportune or
   dangerous moments
– embarrassed by their tears which leak out in inappropriate
   places or with unsympathetic friends
– guilty about their jealousy which is eating their heart out
– addicted to loving a partner who does not reciprocate their
   feeling or who may even abuse it
– crippled by anxiety over the safety of 30-year-old children

Before we move on to looking at how we can control these
kinds of self-destructive emotional habits, let's remember that
the positive woman is not an 'iron lady'. She is, on the contrary, usually highly sensitive and emotional; she often feels
more deeply than people who have trouble controlling their
feelings. In fact, because she is confident of her ability to contain and control, she can open up the emotional throttle to its
full capacity. *In appropriate situations with appropriate people*
she can, for example:

– roar with laughter
– cry her heart out
– shiver and shake with fear
– shout with anger
– make love with passion.

Can you? In my experience increasing numbers of women
can't. Feeling 'too little' used to be the province of men, but
now more and more women are coming for help because they
feel cut off from their emotional selves. Many are nervous and
frightened that their emotions 'will get the better' of them or
that they will 'go over the top'. So, quite understandably, they
aim to keep a tight rein on themselves most of the time. There
are some fairly obvious disadvantages to this:

1. **Stress** – as it is impossible to stop *feeling* as long as we
    are alive and breathing, unless released, our emotions
    become imprisoned in our bodies and play havoc with our
    physical and mental health. In our attempts to suppress

and divert our emotions we can become pill-poppers, alcoholics, gluttons, shopaholics, gamblers and even workaholics! (For the full horror picture see the section on stress, pp. 110–13).

2. **Boredom** – this occurs when we tend to avoid people and situations where we are likely to feel deeply. We may switch off the television during programmes that are 'moving', for fear of being overwhelmed by sadness or nostalgia, turn our backs on the man who makes our heart skip two beats because we fear the grief if we should lose him, turn down the exciting and challenging job because we fear the anxiety that comes with the package. In other words, we can seriously limit our opportunities and deny ourselves the ecstasy of life as well as its pains.

3. **Loss of energy** – both the above eat up energy which could otherwise be used in much more positive ways.

So whether your problem is one of feeling too much or too little, use this following section to give your emotional self a 'service check'. I have chosen to focus on four common emotions – fear, grief, jealousy and anger – which many women find difficult to manage.

Fear

> Life is either a daring adventure or nothing.
>
> HELEN KELLER

When it comes to managing fear the majority of men generally have a head start over women. Their training for masculinity from an early age puts them in situations where they are openly confronted with fear on a repeated basis. Even today, it's little boys rather than girls who are usually shouted at, have their shins 'accidentally' kicked, and are goaded into daring exploits. They still receive more of the violent 'action man' style toys and the thrilling war stories. Their heroes are generally men of fearless courage who serve as models from whom they can learn some coping skills.

Little girls, by contrast, are not exposed to the same 'toughening up processes'. Of course many have terrifying experiences (just look at the figures for child abuse), but how often are girls encouraged to master their fear and soldier on or fight back? Even if their terror is acknowledged, more often than not they are taught to either avoid the danger which produces it or demand protection. So very many girls, in spite of tremendous efforts on the part of parents and teachers to defeat gender stereotyping, reach adult life ridiculously unprepared for its threats and dangers. Understandably, they find the competitive, unprotected adult world terrifying rather than challenging. Is it any wonder that so many women become crippled with anxiety, depression and uncontrollable panic attacks? Or that many others choose to lead uneventful, rather bland lives because they can't cope with the fear that inevitably accompanies a more challenging lifestyle?

> Security is when everything is settled, when nothing can happen to you; security is denial of life.
> GERMAINE GREER

So how can we learn to take more control over this troublesome emotion?

CONTROLLING FEAR

Step 1: Face the Facts About Fear

> Courage is resistance to fear, mastery of fear, not absence of fear.
> MARK TWAIN

Many women may need to get acquainted with some basic truths about fear which, in my experience, the majority of men in our culture seem to take for granted.

Fear Is Essentially Positive

Fear is nature's way of alerting us to external danger and giving us vital extra 'fighting' power. It increases our heart rate, speeds up our breathing to give us an extra boost of oxygen and pumps energy-producing adrenalin into our bloodstream. The fact that we may perceive many 'something and nothing' situations as dangerous is our responsibility. Fear can be friend as well as foe!

> The only difference between fear (a supposedly negative emotion) and excitement (a reputedly positive emotion) is what we choose to call it. The sensation is just the same. We just add a little 'Oh no!' to fear and a little 'Oh boy!' to excitement, that's all.
>
> JOHN ROGER and PETER MCWILLIAMS

The Experience of Fear Is Unavoidable

Because living itself is such an unpredictable business, trying to avoid feelings of fear is fruitless. This must be especially true today when the world and the individuals in it are changing so fast. All forms of change are risky and all risk produces fear – *including personal development*, however positive the goal!

Fear of Fear Can Be More Disabling than Fear Itself

The physical experience of fear – the thumping heart, shaking hands and uncontrollable sweating – terrifies so many women that they try to deny the existence of the danger which might set off such a reaction. They kid themselves (and their children?) that everybody is 'nice', that every cloud has a silver lining, that the hero or heroine will win out, that if we keep busy nothing awful will happen. But their unconscious is not fooled; the buried fright continues to seethe and bubble below the surface until one day the lid is blown – and the worst that could happen happens. The body has a massive uncontrollable defensive reaction – the first panic attack arrives. This terrifying experience becomes associated with whatever the last straw on the camel's back was, whatever the mini-worry became the trigger, or with whatever or whoever just happened to be around at the time. So the roots of a phobia or obsession are sown, leading to more dangers to fear and more negative habits to break!

Fear Can Be Controlled

Even if you cannot control the dangers you have to face, you can be mistress of your reactions to them. This is an area where mind very obviously can triumph over matter. We do not have to be our body's slave. This means that we can learn to take responsibility for our reaction to frightening events and people. The true statement is not 'It was too frightening' but 'I was too frightened.'

Learning to Master Fear Can Be Both Exciting and Energizing

This seems to be one of the main reasons why so many people (mainly men, of course) over and over again voluntarily and unnecessarily take themselves into situations of risk and danger.

Step 2: Learn More About Your Own Fear

Firstly, this means examining your fears in some detail, getting to know their triggers and which ones give you the most trouble in what circumstances, at what time and in whose company, and so on.

Secondly, it means looking at the way you handle your fears. I accept that this part may not be essential but very many people have found that it can help. If possible, take on the major responsibility for this discovery yourself – after all, only you have experienced your world from the unique position of your shoes.

Looking out at the world from the top of the Eiffel Tower may be an absolutely terrifying experience for one person, exciting for another and plain boring to someone else. It is important not to dismiss these differences lightly, with an 'it takes all sorts' reaction. There are many reasons for the differences and one small one might be genetic inheritance, but far more significant are the factors over which we can have some control.

Factors Affecting Our Handling of Frightening Experiences

- **our legacy of our childhood learning**. Were we over-protected or under-protected? Were Mum and Dad cowards or heroes? (We considered the importance of these individual experiences in some detail earlier.)
- **our current emotional state**. If we are feeling on top of the world ourselves, the view from the Eiffel Tower is more likely to appeal rather than daunt.
- **our inner confidence and self-esteem**. We all know that when we are feeling good about ourselves, the world no longer seems such a scary place.
- **our physical health**. I know that when I am suffering from a mild attack of 'flu or I am overtired, I do feel much more vulnerable.
- **our ability to take care of ourselves**. This may include our knowledge of self-defence, first-aid, financial means, knowledge of a place – or even the ability to speak or understand a language. I know that I anticipate feeling anxiety over tackling problems in Spain which I know I can handle with my eyes shut in England and with one hand behind my back in France.
- **our history of exposure to such experiences**. If life has offered you many opportunities to view the world from great heights you may have become desensitized to your fears.
- **our ability to relax our bodies**. If we have been taught the skill of knowing what to do when we first sense the racing of our pulse, we will obviously feel much less afraid because we are not frightened by the fear itself.
- **our support**. If there is a hand to hold sometimes we don't even notice the fear.

EXERCISE: MY FEAR

*List 10 of your fears, including some very big ones and some little
ones. Include some fantasies as well as the more everyday experiences. For the moment don't bother to put them down in any
order of terror – just note them down as they occur to you. Note
the common triggers for these fears and, using the above list,
identify one or two possible causes.*

*When you have finished this part of the exercise, try grading
the fears in order of the amount of anxiety they produce in you or
would produce in you if you did experience them.*

Examples:

Fear	Triggers	Causes
Being lonely	*Someone is late*	*I spent too much*
	Large cities	*time on my own as*
	Arguments with	*a kid*
	friends	*I don't like my*
		own company
Ageing	*Seeing grey hairs*	*My mother died young*
	Being ill	*Financial insecurity*
		I'm not very fit

Step 3: Take Some Positive Action

> To conquer fear is the beginning of
> wisdom.
>
> BERTRAND RUSSELL

What kind of action you take
will depend very much on
what fears you identified in the
last exercise. I am not suggesting that individuals can take
full responsibility for protecting themselves against many of
the very real threats of violence that there are around. As
someone who has been raped on a couple of occasions, I know
only too well how powerless a woman actually can be in certain very frightening situations. But here are just a few of the

things you can do to build up your general resistance to fear and take control of your panic in very many circumstances.

- Do some confidence building and/or Assertiveness Training.
- Buy or borrow books on overcoming fear and biographies of inspirational women.
- Take relaxation or meditation classes.
- Learn self-defence – there are many courses now specifically targeted at women. You do not have to be a fitness freak to join one! I wish I had known some of the simple techniques my daughter recently demonstrated when I was 17.
- Practise positive thinking when facing a fearful situation, and use positive language to help you. For example:
  'This is an exciting adventure.'
  'This is an opportunity for me to gain strength.'
  'I can control my fear.'
  'People are supportive.'

> You gain strength and courage and confidence by every experience in which you really stop to look fear in the face.
> ELEANOR ROOSEVELT

- Use creative visualization to help yourself cope with situations (see Chapter 13).
- Use a step-by-step approach to make changes and take some risks, remembering that all change brings with it some fear. Experiment with small changes which are not too anxiety-provoking. After rewarding yourself, gradually move on to taking risks which make you a little more fearful (e.g. change of hairstyle – doing an advanced driving course – changing job – joining a dating agency). Take one risk or change at a time and don't look too far ahead.

> I have a new philosophy. I'm only going to dread one day at a time.
> CHARLES SCHULZ:
> 'PEANUTS' CARTOON

- Get some support – find friends or a counsellor who will encourage you and not keep emphasizing the 'dangers' and the 'hassle'. Remind yourself not to discuss your fears with negative thinkers! Join a self-help group for people overcoming fears and phobias.
- Support community initiatives designed to protect women and other members of society who may be prone to violent attacks. (These might be better street lighting, women-only car parks, neighbourhood watch schemes or more night police patrols.)

> To go beyond fear we have to accept ourselves and to let other people be themselves and to accept them as they are ... to go beyond fear we have to accept that we have to take life on trust.
>
> DOROTHY ROWE

Grief

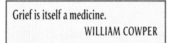

> Grief is itself a medicine.
> WILLIAM COWPER

Grief, like fear, is a positive emotion. It enables us to heal from the inevitable sadness and losses of life. This may seem an obvious truth to some people. If so, they are luckier than the hundreds of women I meet in therapy who do not experience it as positive at all. Some feel devastatingly pained by it – they can talk of nothing else. Others feel a numb resignation – they suffer in silence. All are in some way immobilized by it– they are not moving forward and growing through it. They are stuck in a despair which has a negative effect not just on their own health and life but also on the people around them, including perhaps their own children.

The roots of the problem are various and it certainly doesn't follow that the greater the loss the greater the grief, or the greater the immobility. Here are some examples of the different kinds of losses which can trouble us; some you will notice are more obviously in need of being mourned than others:

the loss of:

- a loved one through death, divorce or separation
- friends through a move or disagreement
- a loved pet
- job through redundancy or retirement
- health through illness, accident or old age
- status or a role such as that of mother, boss
- a loved object
- self-image due to disfigurement
- sight or hearing
- a lifestyle through financial problems, motherhood or divorce
- a part of self, e.g. creativity, sexuality, intellect.

Let's look for a moment at the process of grief if it is able to take its natural positive healing course. It is now well recognized that there are some major phases that we need to pass through in order to recover from loss.

THE PHASES OF BEREAVEMENT

1. **Shock** – experienced as a sense of numbness, abnormal calm, withdrawal, unreality, detachment, inability to express emotions. ('It hasn't really hit me yet.' 'I'm just going around in a daze.')
2. **Denial** – acting as though no loss had occurred. In severe grief the bereaved can experience hallucinations and be convinced that they are hearing their loved one's voice.
3. **Depression** – despair, pain, crying, moaning, wanting to 'give up'.
4. **Guilt** – here the bereaved wonder what they did wrong and wish they had done something differently. ('I wish I hadn't spoken to him like that before he went out.' 'If I hadn't been so demanding ...' 'I should have worked harder.')
5. **Anxiety** – panic about implications of loss. ('I'll never be able to replace him/her/it.' 'I'll never be able to get another job.')

6. **Anger** – feeling victimized and trying to find someone or something to blame. ('It's not fair.' 'Why me?')

7. **Acceptance** – letting go, saying good-bye, appreciating, forgiving – and moving on with hope.

COPING WITH GRIEF

Why do so many people find this natural grieving process so difficult? Why do they seem to get stuck in one or other of these phases? The reasons are various – some cultural, some situational and some personal:

- The culture may expect women (usually more than men) to stay in a permanent, or very extended, state of mourning. Widows (or divorcees) in the West may not be expected to wear black for the rest of their lives, but they are 'expected' to respect the lost person by mourning for a 'decent' amount of time. But who defines decent? The decline in accepted rituals for mourning is confusing to many bereaved people, and indeed their friends, who may perhaps continue to treat them with 'kid gloves' for far longer than they need or try to distract them out of their sadness before it is fully expressed.
- Powerful childhood models may not have approved of grieving ('stiff-upper lip' philosophy) or demonstrated an unhealthy way of working through it (e.g. hanging on to their misery).
- Life may be so busy and fraught that there is no time to grieve properly; practical problems must take precedence.
- There may be a lack of support from others. Perhaps because of their own difficulties and preoccupations, they may feel uncomfortable or irritated at seeing someone 'moping around'. And then because they are feeling especially vulnerable, the bereaved person may feel obliged to 'please'.
- The current loss may have triggered off old unexpressed grief from as far back as childhood and the bereaved may be unaware of this happening, or try to push it away

because the pain is too overwhelming, or feel 'silly' about bringing up the past.

- The personality of the bereaved may render them more vulnerable to getting stuck at one stage of the grieving process. Perhaps they 'need' to feel guilty, can't get angry, find crying difficult, etc.
- The bereaved's feelings about the lost object or person may not have been straightforward. A half-loving, half-hating relationship would result in confusion – not knowing whether to cry or jump for joy.
- The bereaved may be suffering from a lack of self-esteem and self-confidence, which makes any transition difficult.
- Or there may be a lack of motivation – the bereavement may be an 'excuse' for sticking in a depressed position. In this case, the *real* problem may have more to do with not wanting to be successful, make new friends, remarry, be independent – or even live or feel.

I tell you hopeless grief is passionless.
ELIZABETH BARRETT BROWNING

A positive woman must be able to grieve readily and healthily – this is an essential life-skill. As you have been reading this section, you may have found yourself identifying with either some of the losses mentioned or some of the reasons for not being able to grieve efficiently.

I sat a long time upon a stone at the margin of the lake and after a flood of tears my heart was easier.
DOROTHY WORDSWORTH, after losing brothers William and John

If so, it would be worth spending some time looking at your own pattern of dealing with losses, so that you will be better prepared to cope positively with others which will inevitably confront you some time in the future.

Jealousy

> Happiness is beneficial to the body, but it is grief that develops the powers of the mind.
>
> MARCEL PROUST

In our society, jealousy and its 'sister' feeling of envy are probably the most difficult emotions to own up to honestly. This is because they give rise to all sorts of other uncomfortable and socially unacceptable emotions. When we are jealous, we can feel humiliated, left out, abandoned, inferior, suspicious, bitter, resentful, angry and unforgiving, and our behaviour can become over-possessive, unnecessarily competitive, revengeful, unjust, childish, obsessive and compulsive. Neither list has a positive ring to its tone! These emotions can damage our mental stability, our physical health and, of course, our relationships with other people. It's no wonder that we hear ourselves denying their existence: 'I'm not bothered, she can have him if she wants him,' 'I'm happy with my little lot; she can keep her fancy clothes and posh house, for all I care!' But however hard we try and kid ourselves, we may find that our feelings begin to dominate our thoughts and dreams obsessively.

Some forms of jealousy are, of course, more socially acceptable than others, especially for women. We know that if we voice our jealousy of a woman who has robbed us of our man, we are likely to get solidarity from our sisters and possibly a knight on a white charger to right our wrong. If we express envy of the lifestyle of pop stars or the looks of a super-model, we know we are on common ground with others. But if we feel jealous of the platonic girlfriends of that wonderful 'New Man' husband of ours, envious of our loyal best friend, jealous of our children's talents and opportunities or their relationship with their father, what support do we feel we can count on? Indeed, what support do we deserve? So we furiously deny our 'guilty' feelings, or keep them well hidden, and begin to wonder whether we are essentially evil and not 'worthy' of love or success. I know this can happen because I have had this painful experience myself and have heard many women disclose these 'forbidden' feelings in the confidential counselling setting. But, equally, I know that we can learn a good deal about ourselves from confronting these feelings.

> It is the wolf that makes the sheep reflect.
>
> MADAME DE POMPADOUR

CONFRONTING JEALOUSY

Once again the secret is not to blame ourselves for feeling these emotions but rather to focus on ways of learning to keep them under reasonable control. So, how can we break our jealous and envious habits of thought and behaviour? The following are some steps which many people have found useful.

Come Out of the Closet

Own your feelings to the person concerned if they don't already know about them. I know that this is not always possible, but if it is, relief can be found by simply expressing the feeling, and often you may find that it is reciprocated in some way and you can move on to a closer relationship once the rivalry and ambivalence have been acknowledged.

> Rivalry is natural ... the notion that we can feel love and hate at the same time is intimacy's first law.
>
> NANCY FRIDAY

If you are unable to talk to the person concerned, find a trusted friend or counsellor to confide in. You will no doubt hear that you are not alone in your experiences and that feeling of empathy is very supportive when you are trying to change.

Understand the Causes of Your Problem

When these feelings don't 'die a natural death' after being expressed and owned, they probably are not rooted in the relationship which appears to have triggered them off. It is time once again to look in the mirror and your museum of past hurt. Some of the root causes of persistent jealousy and envy can be:

- low self-esteem and conviction of being 'second rate'
- lack of firm sense of identity and needing a 'label' from others (e.g. Mr Jones' wife/'the fairest of them all')
- inability to be emotionally or practically independent
- reluctance to trust
- underlying anger that someone else has the power to make you sad or happy
- boredom with life (jealousy breeds exciting drama!)
- denial of your own right to be successful or happy
- unresolved jealousies and rivalries from childhood
- insufficient unconditional love and security from parents.

> They are not ever jealous for the cause,
> But jealous for they are jealous.
> SHAKESPEARE: OTHELLO

Heal Your Hurt

This may mean a dose of self-nurturing to boost your self-esteem (see Chapter 3) or simply talking through and getting some empathy for the hurt and anger you feel from past relationships. Alternatively, it could mean changing your life very dramatically to allow you to be happy and successful. Assertiveness Training could also help by convincing you of your basic human rights to be seen and heard as much as anyone else.

End Negative Relationships

Many people get a kick out of making other people jealous and envious and will constantly try to hook you back into your old possessive self-destructive patterns. For example, men often get a 'macho boost' just seeing women fight over them, or some women feed their insecure egos by tickling the Achilles heel of your envy. Don't waste your energy trying to make such people change or get revenge on them – leave them. Find more rewarding fish in your sea!

If you find leaving is hard to do, then recognize that you may be addicted to the relationship, just as you can be addicted to smoking, alcohol or chocolate. Get support (from books, friends or a counsellor) to enable you break your habit. Remember to set easy-to-achieve goals for yourself (e.g. 'I won't ring for two days') and then reward yourself at each step along the way.

> Envy shoots at others and wounds herself.
> PROVERB

Once you have broken the back of your addiction, begin to take active steps to find new relationships which will enhance and nurture your positive side.

EXERCISE: BEATING JEALOUSY

1. Name the people who give rise to feelings of jealousy and envy in you.

2. Are your feelings damaging or limiting any of the relationships you have with these people? If so, note down the possible benefits to yourself and the other person if you were to overcome these feelings.

3. Select one or two relationships to discuss with a trusted friend. Explain that you are not asking for advice, merely a chance to air and think through your feelings.

4. Discuss your feelings with the person concerned, taking full responsibility for your feelings and holding back on the accusations. (Don't say, for example, 'You make me feel so jealous.') You may find that the other person admits to consciously or unconsciously feeding your jealousy and you could both discuss changes and strategies which may help you.

5. If the above does not help or you have tried similar actions before, reread the list of root causes of persistent jealousy on page 76 and tick the ones which may apply to you. Using this section on jealousy to help you, formulate an action plan for yourself. Example of an action plan:

   – build up my independence by doing more on my own
   – put more interests into my life, perhaps join a club
   – alter my working life so that I have more chance of success
   – talk to my sister about my childhood feelings of jealousy
   – break the addictive behaviour of checking his movements through using the step-by-step approach and rewarding myself each time there is the slightest hint of progress.

Anger

> Anger is a signal, and one worth listening to. Our anger may be a message that we are being hurt, that our rights are being violated, that our needs or wants are not being adequately met, or simply that something may not be right.
>
> HARRIET GOLDHOR LERNER

Anger is an instinctive response to being frustrated and threatened. It is nature's way of gearing us up physically and mentally to fight. Like fear, it gives us a booster supply of adrenalin, and it makes us feel strong, powerful and motivated to win. Managed *effectively*, anger can both protect and energize us; managed *ineffectively*, like jealousy, it can seriously damage our physical and mental health and destroy our relationships.

In our culture, for many centuries anger has been an emotion which women have been discouraged from both owning and displaying. It did not seem to fit comfortably with the traditional feminine roles of nurturer, peacemaker and mother. Girls growing up would notice that frustrated or angry women were labelled 'naggers', 'fish-wives', 'bitches' and 'shrews'. Their own outbursts would often be mocked and derided or even ignored. As a consequence, they would learn to suppress and deny any hint of such 'negative' feelings in themselves and, moreover, avoid encountering them in anyone else.

Boys, on the other hand, grew up with a very different experience of anger. They were taught that this was one emotion that every 'real man' would, and indeed should, feel. Through teasing, bullying and participation in aggressive sport, parents, teachers and older brothers would actively foster and encourage the boiling of most boys' blood. What happened next would depend on the personal and social background of each boy. The more fortunate would be taught how to control and constructively channel this extra charge of energy, learning how to use anger to empower and protect themselves in the competitive and frustrating world of their adult models. The less fortunate would often be left harmfully seething and become potentially destructive and dangerous (particularly to 'wimps' and women). But whatever route their anger took, boys would at least grow up with an awareness of the existence of this emotion within themselves and a healthy respect for its power and positive potential.

I have been talking in the past tense because I am very aware that cultural stereotypes are fast breaking down, but in my experience it is very evident that this kind of conditioning about anger still exerts considerable power. Too many women still tend to deny feelings of annoyance, irritation and rage; they are too keen to please and too immobilized by others' anger. Many are paying a high price for keeping the peace and 'biting their tongues'. Headaches, pre-menstrual tension and chronic lower back pain are but a few of the most common female complaints that research has now linked with unexpressed frustration and resentment.

Other women, having become convinced of their right to be angry, are finding that the feelings are beginning to surface, but are often disappointed to find themselves 'hitting the wrong target' or getting frighteningly out of control. The danger then is that instead of controlling their anger they may reach too readily for food, cigarettes, alcohol or a dose of tranquilizers to keep themselves cool and calm. As their addiction and consequent self-disgust and depression creeps up, the original frustration and anger is forgotten and lost. *But this negative cycle is not the fault of anger – it is the fault of the mismanagement of anger.*

COPING POSITIVELY WITH ANGER

It is very important for every woman who wants to live positively to be able to handle both her own and other people's anger, and I am convinced that if you can achieve the former, the latter presents few problems. If you feel frightened and overpowered by your own anger, then you are much less able to cope with similar feelings in others.

The first step, as always, is to get to know and understand your own patterns and habits. Do the following exercise and if a significant number of bells start to ring, read on to the end of the chapter!

> Because of the kind of father I had, it was never possible to express my anger, so now I bottle it all up and get very resentful, which is supposed to give you cancer.
>
> SHIRLEY CONRAN

EXERCISE: MY ANGER

Read the following list of some common symptoms of the mismanagement of anger and mark those with which you can identify:

- *becoming the office or family's unofficial peacemaker*
- *playing the lovable clown too often*
- *being the good girl who secretly envies the bad*
- *being the nice girl who everybody loves and apparently never gives rise to aggression in others*
- *going quiet as soon as an argument begins to escalate*
- *feeling upset or surprised because 'they' didn't guess how irritated or annoyed you would be*
- *feeling persistently under-appreciated and 'taken for granted', in spite of your 'niceness'*
- *feeling hurt or always ending up in tears after a disagreement*
- *finding yourself unable to forget a disagreement or annoyance even if the other person has apologized*
- *moaning or maliciously gossiping and 'bitching' behind people's backs*

If the identification bells have been ringing fast and furiously as you read down the list, take heart from my own and many other therapists' experience. It is possible to change these patterns and begin to use your anger in an assertive manner.

> You can learn to express your anger cleanly and directly, without destroying or punishing yourself or anyone else in the process. And in doing so, you can begin to recover a powerful source of vitality, a sense of your own power and energy and identity.
>
> ANN DICKSON

GUIDELINES FOR ASSERTIVE ANGER

Share Your Feelings Directly

Sharing your feelings in a direct way shows both you and others that you are 'in touch' with your feelings and therefore more likely to be in control. Say 'I'm feeling angry/ irritated/ annoyed' and don't distance yourself from the feelings by beating about the bush with indirect statements which may start with 'When people ...' or 'It can be very difficult when ...' or 'In this world we have to ...' Never rely on anyone, however close they are to you, to *guess* what you are feeling.

Don't Accuse Others of *Making You Angry*

No person or situation has the power to *make* you feel anything. Accept that your individual threshold for stress is your responsibility. Say '*I* get irritated when ...' and not '*You* make me irritated.' The latter statement will immediately put others on the defensive and therefore they will be less likely to hear you out.

Don't Play 'Amateur Psychologist'

Avoid making interpretations about the other person's personality and behaviour:

> 'You just wanted to pull me down a peg or two.'
> 'You don't really want to ...'
> 'I know what you are really thinking ...'

or putting them into a 'box' by associating them with others:

> 'You're just like your father.'
> 'It's just your male arrogance ...'
> 'You're the type who always ...'

Share Your Feelings of Fear and Threat

We often hold back on our criticisms because we feel that the other person will reject or hurt us. Often there is a good reason for persistently feeling this – maybe significant people did actually walk away from our anger when we were a child or when we were in another defenceless state. If you say, 'I'm frightened that you'll walk away or hit me if I tell you ...', more often than not you will receive the reassurance that you need – and if you don't then you can choose to keep quiet and take flight!

Give Some Physical Expression to Your Feelings

Don't forget that it's not childish and not 'unfeminine' to stamp your feet, bang doors, throw cushions or scream – in fact, in moderation, it is a sensible way of releasing pent-up tension, and certainly preferable to making threatening gestures to other people. Reassure anyone frightened by your behaviour, though, especially children, that you will not hurt them, however angry you may be.

Obviously if the scene of your angry exchange is the boardroom or even a local supermarket you may choose to curtail the physical expression of your feelings! If you do so, make sure that you have an early opportunity to release your physical tension, otherwise this will be stored in your body and could in the long term harm your health. Some people choose to 'let go' by doing strenuous physical exercise on a regular basis, but you can, in the privacy of your own home, just beat a few cushions while giving voice to your frustrations.

If you find either of these two options doesn't work, or you have a frighteningly large store of pent-up anger, find an experienced therapist or group who will encourage you to 'let off steam' in a safe, supportive atmosphere.

Don't Raid Your 'Museum of Past Grievances'

Avoid 'and while we are at it' jibes; stick to the issue at hand. Accept that it is your own fault if you have stored up a lot of frustration and anger through not assertively dealing with situations as they arise. You can feel very deflated and 'thrown off course' if someone turns around and says 'Well, you should have said something then, shouldn't you?'

If you know that you have lots of stored up anger which doesn't relate to the immediate issue, try to find some way of releasing this before confronting the other person. You could do this by having a good moan to a sympathetic friend or by shouting at a cushion or empty chair. Make a list of these unresolved issues and make arrangements to discuss them calmly and coolly at some other pre-arranged time.

Vow Never Again to Ignore the 'Niggles'

In long-term relationships, deal with each little irritation as it occurs; don't dismiss them as not 'worth making a fuss over' because they could mount up. Dealing with these small issues sets an assertive tone to your relationship and builds up a sense of confidence that it is secure enough to withstand disagreement. In such an atmosphere angry exchanges are less likely to escalate into uncontrollable rage.

Never Threaten 'Punishments' You Cannot or Will Not Enforce

Don't say that you'll resign, sue for divorce, leave your child in the supermarket, call the police, etc., unless you are truly prepared to take these actions, otherwise your anger will be immediately disregarded and will lose its power because you will either have frozen your 'opponent' into a state of terror or you will have made yourself look ridiculous in their eyes.

Don't Involve a Third Party

It is to be hoped that most of us now feel too liberated to use the classic threats that many of us were brought up on – 'I'll get my brother to sort you out' or 'Wait till your father gets home' – but check that you are not doing something similar in a less direct fashion. Some examples of this are:

'Your father would be very disappointed to hear that.'
'You'll break Mum's heart.'
'The boss wouldn't like to hear about ...'
'Everybody else feels the same, you wait and see ...'
'If the police got to hear of this ...'

This kind of manipulative behaviour will depower your anger.

Stick to your own grievances and feelings. If support for your cause is justified, enlist it directly when you have calmed down – but don't use it as a weapon to fight your own battles.

Insist on a Follow-up Discussion

Wait until your physical feelings of anger have settled down before making any attempt to sort out the rights and wrongs of the situation or relationship. Don't be tempted to allow a joke, seductive smile or kiss to make you 'forget that it ever happened' until you have *discussed* the cause of your anger and negotiated some kind of 'settlement'.

Say Sorry, If Necessary

When we are angry we are especially likely to say, and some-times do, all sorts of things that we don't mean. Apologize for anything you truly regret doing or saying, but don't overdo the self-flagellation – 'What an awful person I am!' – and don't say sorry for having *felt* the way you did unless that feeling was actually misplaced.

Express Your Feelings

Even if the problem is insoluble, don't hold back on your anger just because nothing can be done to alter the cause of your hurt and frustration. Maybe you will never be able to get that order you lost, change the company's policy, get back your health, stop your partner loving someone else or make your father respect you, but you still have the *right* to feel the way you do. Express your feelings with someone whom you can trust, and release the physical tension. A show of justified anger will often bring forth invaluable support and healing comfort.

> I don't get overstressed by all the problems – I get angry. Anger is a wonderful emotion. It gets you going.
> CLARE RAYNER

> The positive woman enjoys her emotions and is proud to have them under *her* control.

CHAPTER 6

Kicking Negative Habits of Behaviour

Now that you have begun to tackle your thinking and feeling habits it is important that you do not leave your behaviour behind. A change in attitude will, of course, help transform your life but if you marry it up with a change in behaviour, it will be more than twice as powerful.

The Importance of Our Behaviour

> Behaviour is a mirror in which everyone shows their image.
>
> GOETHE

Before we can break negative habits of behaviour, we must first take the following steps:

ACCEPT THAT WE WILL BE JUDGED BY OUR BEHAVIOUR

This means facing up to a truth which I, along with many others, find very difficult to swallow, and that is that as far as other people are concerned *we are our behaviour*! Yet we may often kid ourselves that it is not so. We make 'excuses' for our behaviour and disassociate it from our 'true selves' because we *know* what we are really like inside. But, due to our behaviour, others may perceive us differently. For example:

- Gill never speaks her mind at staff meetings.
    → Gill is perceived as a person who isn't too bothered about the company policy and the general welfare of others (in spite of the fact that, inwardly, she knows that she lies awake at night worrying about the decisions that have been made).
- Mary threatens her child with a slap.
    → Mary is perceived as a potentially violent mother (in spite of the fact that, inwardly, she knows that she would never hurt a fly).

Of course there will always be people who will put their own subjective interpretation on our behaviour, no matter *what* we do to improve our own communication patterns. We may just have to resign ourselves to being misjudged sometimes – but we can choose to break the habits which are *continually* being negatively misinterpreted.

Firstly, we can make up our minds not to waste precious energy in continually *defending* our misinterpreted behaviour ('I didn't really mean to say/do/give the impression that ...'), but rather vow to *change* it. You can show yourself and others that you mean business by *asking for specific feedback*. For example:

Ask people to clarify what they actually saw or heard when they criticize your behaviour:
'Was my voice too loud?'
'Wasn't I smiling?'
Ask people for regular feedback even if they do not criticize your behaviour. (Sometimes people may be frightened of you, or think you can't take criticism.)
'Do you think I made enough contributions to the meeting?'
'Have I been less irritable this week?'

'Have you heard me putting myself down this week?'
'Have I been more cheerful this week?'

ACCEPT RESPONSIBILITY FOR OUR OWN BEHAVIOUR

This means that, unless we operate within the confines of a torture chamber or there are some other very unusual mitigating circumstances, we must stop blaming others or difficult situations for our own action or non-action! This means catching ourselves saying or thinking such things as:

'He made me do it – it was the way he looked at me.'
'If she hadn't done that, I wouldn't have been tempted.'
'If you weren't such a drip, I wouldn't have to shout at you all the time.'

and considering what we really mean. Only when we accept the importance of *our own* behaviour and take full responsibility for it can we be truly motivated to begin the difficult (but not impossible!) task of changing some of the patterns.

Changing Our Behaviour

One of the secrets of changing our behaviour is to *substitute an alternative*. Most parents learn this skill by trial and error. We find out the hard way that you can tell a child over and over again to stop doing something but, unless you suggest an alternative to kicking his sister or drawing on the walls, you are wasting your breath! But then we often forget to use this wisdom on ourselves. We often just order ourselves to stop over-apologizing, nagging, being late, etc., and punish ourselves when we fail to comply. We do not give ourselves a chance to learn new ways of behaving.

The following are some examples of negative patterns and the positive alternatives you can use to help yourself break them.

BEAT MOANING WITH INITIATION

Stop yourself from repeatedly saying:

'If only ...'
'It's not fair ...'
'Yes, but ...'

using a whiny voice, pouting lip or persistent sighing.
Instead, *take alternative action*:

– In front of a mirror, practise talking to yourself about the
  problem, using a lower voice (although you don't have to
  sound like a man!) and checking that your body and face
  look relaxed.
– Make yourself a nurturing drink, sit down comfortably and
  do the following exercise!

EXERCISE: TAKING THE INITIATIVE

*Make a list of some of the 'injustices' and problems you find
yourself persistently bringing up and note in brackets what
actions you could initiate.*
  For example:

My sister always expects me to be at the end of the phone for her	*I could ring her tonight and tell her how much her insensitivity is annoying me.*
	I could ring her when I have a problem
	I could buy an answerphone and use it to monitor calls when I want peace.
Hardly any women have been promoted in this office this year	*I could arrange for the subject to be put on the staff meeting agenda.*
	I could write to the board of directors.

	I could ring equal opportunities organizations for advice and statistics.
No one else in the house cleans the bathroom	I could make a rota.
	I could take a book in with me and stage a 'sit-in' as protest!

Don't wait to be contacted or for the problem or feeling to crop up again – ring, write or knock on the door as soon as you are ready and prepared to act. How many of us swear that we will 'tell them' or 'show them' the next time!

BEAT WORRYING WITH CONTINGENCY PLANNING

> Don't agonize. Organize.
> FLORENCE KENNEDY

If you hear yourself saying repeatedly

'I only hope he doesn't ...'
'I don't know what I'll do if ...'
'I wouldn't know what to do if ...'
'I couldn't cope if ...'

then *take alternative action* and do this exercise.

EXERCISE: CONTINGENCY PLANNING

Ask yourself what are some of the worst scenarios you could face during the next few months and outline some specific contingency plans.

For example:

If I do have to go into hospital, I could	– ask Maureen to pick the children up each day
	– treat myself to a new nightdress and two good books
	– ask to see the welfare officer to sort out sick pay

| If I am made redundant on Monday, I will | – ring Mary and arrange to meet and have a good cry or shout
– ask for some leave to start job-hunting
– ring the bank to check my overdraft facilities and investment options for redundancy pay
– update my CV and send it around. |

You will find in the course of making this kind of plan, it will become obvious that there are many things which can be done immediately and will help divert your attention from your worries. Remember that positive people do not keep their heads in the sand, they combine their optimism with pragmatic planning and preparation.

BEAT INDECISION WITH DECISIVENESS

Perhaps the most important thing that has come out of my life is the discovery that if you prepare yourself at every point as well as you can, with whatever means you have, however meagre they may seem, you will be able to grasp opportunity for broader experience when it appears. Without preparation you cannot do it.

HELENA RUBINSTEIN

Note when you are unnecessarily putting off the evil day when you have to make up your mind or when you give over the responsibility for it too easily to others. Watch out for *repeatedly* saying to yourself or others:

'Just give me until next week.'
'Let me just check it through again.'
'What would you do?'
'You choose.'
'I don't mind.'

Sometimes you may not even be aware of your indecisiveness because it has become such an accepted habit, so ask people to tell you when they think you are pussy-footing or shilly-shallying. In the meantime, firm up your decision-making skills by doing the following:

- Practise, and use, a decision-making technique such as The GEE Strategy or FACE the Facts (see Chapter 4).
- Buy or borrow books on the subject – usually to be found in the 'Business' sections of libraries and bookshops. If the suggestions given don't correspond exactly to what you need, remember they can always be adapted to suit your purposes.
- Practise making quick decisions over low-risk choices, for example, which television programme to watch, which tin of baked beans to buy. Make a note of these in your diary and reward yourself after every 10 decisions you make.
- Make a list of your six key values, and then make a list of your six top priorities, rating them in order of importance. Review your dating decisions in the light of your values.
- Ask yourself if your indecisiveness is partly influenced by anyone else's values or wishes or even the kind of 'unfinished business' we looked at in Chapter 3.
- Make a list of all the good decisions you have made in your life.
- In your kitchen or office, pin up a positive affirmation such as 'I am able to act decisively.'
- Remind yourself of your *right* to make mistakes, and then act!

> What the hell - you might be right, you might be wrong - but don't just avoid.
> KATHERINE HEPBURN

BEAT BOOT-LICKING WITH CHALLENGE AND CONFRONTATION

> She was nothing more than a mere good-tempered and obliging young woman; as such we could scarcely dislike her - she was only an object of contempt.
>
> JANE AUSTEN

Even if you don't think of yourself as someone who curries favours or fawns at people's feet, perhaps you know that you:

– are guilty of not being able to say 'no' to certain people
– 'sweeten up' others to stop them getting angry with you or ultimately rejecting you
– find yourself buying things just to please the salesperson
– or doing unnecessary cleaning to avoid the family's criticisms.

All these are ingratiating forms of behaviour which can have very negative effects both on your self-esteem and your identity. Doormats are reliable and useful, but who notices them, who bothers to clean or care for them, who sheds a tear when they are worn away?

If you want to develop skills which will enable you to defend your rights and demand that your needs be given the same priority as other people's, try this exercise:

EXERCISE: REFUSING THE BAIT

Write down an example of an assertive refusal for a request for help, using the technique called 'Broken Record'. The idea of this technique is that you choose a key sentence which directly and simply states what you will or will not do and then in a calm, controlled voice, you can respond to each question or statement by simply repeating the heart of this sentence.

Practise responding to all the arguments and emotional blackmail which normally 'hook' into your ingratiating habit, and make a note in brackets of the bait which is being used – this will help you to face the reality of the manipulation and keep you on track with your assertiveness! For example:

Hannah:	*'Would you mind being an angel and making the tea after you have finished that report?' (Bait = I will think you are a lovely person if you do!)*
Jo:	*'I've made the tea four times already this week and I'm not prepared to do it again.'*
Hannah:	*'Oh go on, it won't take a minute, I've got three meetings this afternoon.' (Bait = You're such a nice person – I know that you will feel sorry for me!)*
Jo:	*'No, I've made the tea four times this week and I'm not prepared to do it again.'*
Hannah:	*'You're the only one around here whom I can rely on to help out.' (Bait = You're nicer than anybody else!)*
Jo:	*'No, I'm not prepared to make the tea again.'*
Hannah:	*'What's got into you today – why are you being so difficult?' (Bait = I won't like you if you are not nice!)*
Jo:	*'I've made the tea four times already this week and I'm just not prepared to make it again.'*

(You can find a fuller explanation of Broken Record and examples of how it can be used in other situations in my earlier books Assert Yourself *and* Super Confidence.*)*

BEAT AGGRESSION WITH AWARENESS AND ASSERTION

> Aggressive behaviour is not unalterable; on the contrary, it is one of the most flexible and widely varying aspects of the social lives of animals and people.
>
> JOHN KLAMA

In writing this section, I am making the assumption that you are not a person who maliciously sets out to hurt and depower other people, but that you do have some habits which are perceived as aggressive and therefore will get a negative reaction. People often use 'put-down' language without realizing that in so doing they are abusing the rights of another person.

Very many women have never been adequately taught how to stand up for their rights or put their point across forcefully. Through our cultural conditioning, we may have learned (as I certainly did!) how to exert influence through manipulative and subtle means which did not appear to threaten our safety and 'sweetness'. Then, with the arrival of Women's Liberation and feminism and an awakening of a sense of power, we began to use aggressive behaviour which we perceived as powerful. Many of us simply did not realize that there was a third alternative until Assertiveness Training began to open our eyes. The strategies and techniques we learned then showed us how our needs and wants could be communicated while still respecting other people's basic human rights. Making plain our own needs while respecting those of others is what we should continue to strive for.

Assertive behaviour cannot always guarantee positive reactions because there will always be bullies around who feed off other people's aggression and passivity, but it usually does win out in the end, and we certainly feel much better about ourselves when we use it. There are now many books and courses readily available to help you understand and practise assertiveness, but here is an exercise you can do immediately which will get you moving in the right direction. If you open a conversation assertively, you are much more likely to be able to continue in that mode and are more likely to command the full attention of those you are speaking to.

EXERCISE: ASSERTIVE COMMUNICATION

Read the following list and, using some of the (assertive) openings, compose 10 statements or questions which are relevant to your life and relationships. Practise reading them in front of a mirror using matching (assertive) non-verbal clues.

VERBAL OPENERS

'I' statements and requests
- *I would like you to ...*
- *I feel that ...*
- *I think that ...*
- *I don't want to ...*
- *I will not ...*
- *I cannot ...*

Co-operative statements and questions
- *Let's see what everyone else thinks ...*
- *What do you want ...*
- *How can we resolve this ...*
- *Let's discuss ...*
- *Shall we negotiate ...*
- *Have you any suggestions ...*

Empathic statements
- *I appreciate that it is difficult for you ...*
- *I can see that you seem worried ...*
- *You may be too busy now, but ...*
- *I understand that this may not be something which is very important to you, but ...*

NON-VERBAL ACCOMPANYING BEHAVIOUR
- *Calm purposeful walk*
- *Upright posture with weight evenly balanced on two feet*
- *Relaxed hands and legs (not clenched or tightly crossed)*
- *Direct eye contact (but not glaring)*
- *Strong, clear, steadily-paced voice*
- *Expressive face and gestures (but no fidgeting)*
- *Relaxed, non-manipulative smiling, as appropriate.*

BEAT SHYNESS WITH SOCIABILITY AND CHEERFULNESS

> Life becomes useless and insipid when we have no longer either friends or enemies.
> QUEEN CHRISTINA OF SWEDEN

Not every positive woman has to be an extrovert, highly gregarious creature, but perhaps you have acquired habits of behaviour which mean that you seem more introverted than either you would like to be, or is appropriate for the social circle and work environment that you want to be in. Answer the following questions to check your sociability.

- Do you often make excuses for not joining in or going out?
- Are you so absorbed in or committed to your work that there is never time for a social life?
- Are you in anyone else's shadow?
- Are your friends your own or are they your partner's, brother's, family's?
- Do you feel a bit lost when you are out of your professional role or uniform?
- Do you find the conversation going on all around you?
- Are all, or most, of your hobbies solitary?
- Do you tend to wait for others to make the first move?
- Do you blush or suffer from other physical symptoms of anxiety when you are with people?
- Do you find that you often miss the joke?
- Do people think you are too solemn and serious?
- Do you frequently feel lonely?

If you have answered 'yes' to the majority of these questions then it might be useful for you to plan a programme for yourself which will give you an opportunity to practise some social skills. You could:

- **Practise initiating conversation.** Start in low-risk situations, which are usually in places where you are likely to remain anonymous, for example the supermarket queue, the beach or the petrol station. When you have gained some confidence, start to practise at work or in the local gym or bar.

- **Practise listening.** I have already referred to the skill of 'Reflection' (see page 44), and if you manage to acquire this skill, people will seek you out as a friend!

- **Use empathy statements** such as those listed above – people will love you even more for using these!

- **Watch for non-verbal clues to feelings** but don't confront the person unless you are very close to them. (You can practise this skill by people-watching in the train or in restaurants and seeing how many 'guesstimates' about their feelings you can make. This is a very old habit of mine which drives my husband mad, but I can justify it as it keeps my observation skills in good working order!)

- **Use self-disclosure.** Start being a little more open about what you are feeling and what is happening in your life. Self-disclosure encourages other people to open up and brings relationships on to a more intimate level. (You can start by giving voice to your feelings of anxiety or embarrassment and these will then often miraculously vanish!)

- **Smile freely** – but not meekly.

- **Keep small talk general at first.** Don't ask probing or personal questions until you have built up some trust.

- **Make a habit of telling people all your good news** – and ask them about theirs. Be direct but general, for example: 'Did you go anywhere nice this week-end?' 'Did you watch anything good on television last night?'

- **Use open-ended questions** if you want to keep a conversation going. These are likely to give you more than a 'yes' or 'no' answer.

- **Collect funny stories and witty remarks to recount** – but avoid standard jokes, cynicism and self-deprecation.

- **Become playful** – but avoid being coy or playing practical jokes. Both have a habit of backfiring.

- **Use your imagination.** When you feel yourself slipping into your 'too serious' mood, take a mental step back and try to imagine what a humorous friend of yours might say at this point – or indeed what sort of material the situation could provide for comediennes like Jenny Eclair, Donna McPhail, Dawn French, Jennifer Saunders or Victoria Wood.

> Even if you are on the right track you'll get run over if you just sit there.
> ANON

BEAT ADDICTION WITH CONSIDERED CHOICE

Very few of us can boast to being completely free of addictions of one kind or another and most of us might confess to several which we would prefer not to have in our lives. Some people's addictions are very chronic and may have the added complication of physical dependency. These are not the type of addictions which a short section in a book like this can hope to address – they usually require long-term help from either skilled professionals or self-help groups of ex-addicts. This discussion is intended to help people with more minor difficulties which in themselves are not seriously life-threatening or likely to be the major cause of a major personal or social catastrophe. The following are common examples, some of which will no doubt ring a few bells.

- Eating certain kinds of foods too often, such as chocolate, cream cakes, biscuits – or even salad!
- Obsessively trying each new diet or slimming food which comes onto the market even though you are only slightly overweight.
- Compulsively shopping for dresses, knick-knacks, food or make-up which you don't need and maybe don't even want.
- Watching too many soap operas, game shows or news broadcasts.
- Double-checking the security of the house before leaving it each day.
- Obsessively cleaning the house, car, office or garden.

- Picking and prodding spots or other physical imperfections.
- Compulsively ringing an 'old flame' or surreptitiously trying to find out what he or she is now up to.
- Indulging in sexual rituals which leave you feeling demeaned or disgusted with yourself.

These kind of addictions may never rise to such proportions that they take you to the psychiatrist's chair, but you know that you want to be more in control of them because they perhaps:

   – damage your self-esteem
   – use up too much emotional, mental or physical energy
   – cause offence and annoyance and often give rise to
     arguments
   – stop you from feeling as fit as you would like to feel
   – prevent you from looking as good as you would like to look
   – leave you with less money than you need or want.

As you think about the behaviour, note what you are feeling. It may give you a clue about the root cause of the addiction. There is usually a 'pay-off' for even the silliest of addictions. It may be that doing what you do makes you feel temporarily more important, useful, kinder or glamorous. Alternatively doing whatever you are doing may stop you from feeling unpleasant feelings or making decisions and changes that you need to make.

Jo was working as a lab assistant for a large pharmaceutical company. She had developed a bad habit of going to bed at least one hour later than she needed to. As a result of a New Year's resolution, she broke this habit. But by spring she had developed a new one – being late in for work! During some counselling sessions for an entirely different problem, she mentioned this bad habit. It then emerged that Jo was not at all happy in her job. It was one that she had 'drifted' into after being turned down for one that she had really wanted. She

➤

realized that it would be self-sabotaging to 'force the issue' by behaving in such a way that she might be given notice for this job. (The apparent pay-off for her bad habits was that someone else would make the decision of her!) Instead she decided to seek some career advice so she could find a job which would motivate her to get up in the mornings and have a good night's sleep!

Cheryl is a sales manager for a software company. She had developed a habit of skipping her lunch hour, just eating a sandwich on the way to her next client or meeting. After a consultation with her doctor about her increasing migraines, she decided to take this habit in hand and take an hour out of the office in a local café. At first she would read a magazine or a novel over lunch, but very soon she found herself searching for a table in the café where she had enough space to set up her lap-top!

It was only after a series of severe migraine attacks, which kept her off work for almost a week, that she decided to look more deeply for the root cause of her workaholism. She accepted that she had replaced one self-destructive habit with another. At heart she knew that her basic problem was that she was lonely, but she didn't want anyone else to take pity on her and had not put making friends anywhere near the top of her agenda. The 'pay-off' for keeping herself so busy was either avoiding being in social situations at lunchtime or being seen to be on her own not needing the company of anyone else.

After some reflection she realized that since she'd been promoted to manager she had gradually become isolated in the office. She decided that she would make an effort to ensure her team had more social time together with her, and that she would also invite other managers to have lunch with her.

EXERCISE: BEATING ADDICTION

- *Face up to the fact that you are addicted. You can do this by making some kind of 'public' declaration to friends or a member of your family. Pin a notice on your wall to confront yourself daily with the reality and only take it down when you have truly broken the habit.*

- *Stop kicking yourself for having the addiction. Replace self put-downs with positive statements like:*

  'I'm so childish.' → *'I will behave more maturely next time.'*
  'I'm a fanatic for ...' → *'I often like to ...'*
  'I'm hopeless, I'll never be able to ...' → *'I have persistence and will not give up trying to ...'*
  Ask someone close to you to tell you when you use negative talk about yourself.

- *Make a list of reasons for breaking this habit and preface it with the statement 'I am choosing not to ... because ...' Read it just before going to bed and also first thing in the morning for a week. Finish each reading with a positive affirmation. For example:*
  - *I am choosing not to eat biscuits with my coffee*
  - *I care about my health*
  - *I am choosing not to put the TV on every night*
  - *I value my relationship and enjoy having more time to talk to my partner*
  - *I am choosing not to double check that the children have finished their homework*
  - *I enjoy the freedom that giving the children more responsibility gives me.*

- *Make a note of any hidden pay-off you may be getting from this habit. If you identify one, decide what you could do to satisfy your need in a less destructive way.*

- *Do not invite punishment. Stop saying things like*
  'You think I am really silly, don't you?'
  'You've a right to shout at me, go on ...'
  'You'll be so disappointed in me – I did ... again today.'

- *Ask for praise and encouragement. Make a direct request such as:*
  'Don't you think I did well?'
  'Give me a hug because today I haven't once ...'
- *Congratulate and/or treat yourself each time you have achieved some success, however minor, and promise yourself a major reward when you have been free of the habit for several months.*

The positive woman chooses to act in a responsible and self-supporting manner.

TWO

Getting

Equipped

CHAPTER 7

Improving Your Physical Well-being

Health is not valued till sickness comes.
PROVERB

An essential part of any positive woman's equipment is a body which is running to its maximum efficiency. We need as much physical energy as we can get as well as that extra mental boost that a feeling of vitality can give us. In the last few chapters we have mentioned the stressful effect of negative thoughts, feelings and behaviour on the body, but it is also important to look at the coin from the opposite side. **Physical well-being can help us to think, feel and behave more positively.** So in this chapter, we will consider ways in which we can improve our fitness, take advantage of the preventative health measures available and cope positively with illness, handicap and old age.

Keeping Fit

The vast majority of my clients when they first come to see me are not only feeling and behaving negatively, they are invariably very unfit. They look pale and tired, tend to be over or underweight, and more often than not are suffering from an endless stream of viral infections and chronic aches and pains. One of my first tasks is to confront them with this reality, because often they have simply not noticed! Perhaps they have been too preoccupied and stressed to give their body the time and attention it deserves, or perhaps because their self-esteem is so low, looks in the mirror have been kept to a minimum. If they *have* noticed, they tend to feel so ashamed and guilty that it is often difficult to get them to even talk about their body or health. They know that they have allowed themselves to slip into many bad habits, but they don't feel they have the energy, let alone the motivation, to break them.

I have no trouble at all in empathizing with this sort of state because I can recall being in a similar position many times in my life. I am still no 'fitness freak' and cannot imagine the day when I might become one, but I do know that I have more energy and vitality than I did when I was in my twenties, merely because I do now love myself and my life enough to take much better care of my body. Although I do have to bring in the rescue services when the warning lights of flab, spots, and catarrh start flashing, generally I keep in 'good enough shape' to be able to do what I want to do with my life. The aim of this section is to provide a checklist to help you achieve a similar standard of imperfection; if you want more, you must turn to the experts!

IS YOUR DIET GOOD ENOUGH?

Most women know without checking the scales whether they eat too much or too little, but can you also vouch for the *quality* of your intake? In spite of increasing 'food scares', regular articles in magazines on nutrition and the new labelling on food, I am still amazed by the ignorance I regularly encounter.

So, firstly, do you feed your metabolism with a good balance of vitamins, minerals, protein and fibre? You probably don't if you suffer regularly from the following common complaints:

- dry flaking skin
- brittle nails
- a very red tongue
- bleeding gums
- dull lifeless hair
- thrush
- pre-menstrual tension
- colds and throat infections
- migraine-type headaches
- tiredness

If you identified with several of the above, you can immediately start to establish better eating patterns by:

- reducing your level of animal fat intake; switching over from red meat to poultry, fish or vegetarian proteins such as nuts and lentils
- eating more fresh vegetables; steaming or microwaving rather than boiling, if you want to cook them
- increasing your intake of other fibre through eating whole grains and beans
- reducing your intake of sugar and salt
- cutting down on caffeine, alcohol, smoking and unnecessary antibiotics and other medications
- avoiding prepared foods and seasonings containing harmful additives
- cut down on the foods your body does not tolerate well. Red wine, cheese, yeast extract and chocolate gives rise to high levels of histamine in the brain and should be avoided by migraine sufferers
- taking a daily multi-vitamin tablet, but more importantly checking your diet each week against a table of vitamins and minerals. These can be found in any good book on nutrition. Most people should not need extra supplements if their intake of food is balanced. You are probably already aware of the research which now indicates that many people have been overdosing on vitamin supplements.

Needless to say, if these basic self-help tips have little effect over a period of several months, ask your doctor to give you a physical check-up and possibly refer you to a nutritionist.

ARE YOU GETTING ENOUGH EXERCISE?

My automatic response to this question is invariably 'no'. I have about 40 years' experience of avoiding exercise and know *every* variation of excuse and rationalization. The crazy thing is that I actually enjoy many forms of exercise, but the idea of it always feels like a 'chore'. My bad habits and negative attitudes started in school, as they often do, in response to sadistic PE teachers, gruelling cross-country runs, cold showers and highly competitive peers. Many subsequent hours of swimming in beautiful warm pools and having exciting squash confrontations and friendly badminton knock-ups have failed to obliterate these memories. I still need to discipline myself to take regular healthy exercise, but I won't give up because I want good health and longevity.

The good news for people like me is that recent research would indicate that we need less exercise than many of us have always thought. I no longer have to feel guilty about not taking a daily jog as I understand that according to current medical opinion we can get by quite easily on *three half-hour periods of exercise per week*, as long as the activity is regular, strenuous enough to increase our pulse rate and bring us out in a light sweat, and exercises enough muscles to keep us reasonably supple. But, of course, if you can find an activity which is also fun, increases your circle of friends, gives you a dose of fresh air, tones up your muscles and helps you release pent-up tension, you could gain even extra vitality and stamina by doing it every day!

Are You Stressed?

Stress is the name we have attributed to the negative effects of having more pressure in our lives than we can manage. For

➤

very many years, therapists have been warning people about the potential damage it can do, not only to health but also to our ability to work, drive carefully, budget efficiently and be a good parent or lover. At last the world is taking notice, firstly because there have been many research projects which have proved the point, but secondly because stress no longer affects just a minority of vulnerable people – it has become a problem for the majority of us. This is particularly true for women, most of whom are juggling several different 'lives' and responsibilities.

But let's not forget that having too little pressure in your life can also lead to stress. Boredom, disappointment and envy (which were common emotions felt by pre-liberated women) can also drain our energy and cause many problems similar to those experienced by a workaholic jet-setting executive. In recent years I have been working with many stressed high achievers in the business world, and find that their personal concerns and feelings are no different from the grossly under-achieving women with whom I worked during my early days as a social worker for a mental health charity.

The secret everyone is looking for is, of course, how to maintain a balance. We need to know how to give ourselves enough pressure so that we are excited and motivated, but not so much that we become stressed. Unfortunately there is no quick, pat, golden set of rules I can give you. We each have to find our own unique sense of balance. The amount of pressure each of us can manage depends on two main factors:

1. **Our personality** – if we are lively, extrovert and ambitious then we will probably fare better with quite high levels of pressure, but if we are more introverted and cautious we might well become over-anxious under the same amount. So self-knowledge is once again very important. Being aware of the kind of person you really are will help you to plan your lifestyle so that you can have just the right amount of pressure to keep you energized and motivated. Of course, to achieve this you also need the self-confidence to be yourself and refrain from constantly

comparing your style, achievements and values with others.

2. **Our powers of recuperation** – pressure does put strain on our body's resources and we can take much more of it if we know how to recharge our system. There are many hundreds of ways of doing this, from taking the dog for a walk to transcendental meditation.

   In a recent book *Positive Under Pressure* which I jointly authored with Dr Malcolm VandenBurg, we have included a wide variety of pressure-management techniques. Some of these are my own favourites, while others are ones which have never worked for me but which I know have transformed the lives of many other people. It's all a matter of experimenting until you find the unique individual recipe which suits your personality and lifestyle.

   Basically, you are looking for an activity or technique which helps you switch off your mental high and calms your pulse. The deeper the relaxation, the more quickly you can be recharged. Many busy people are turning to self-hypnosis and meditation because these can take them quickly to that very healing 'floaty' state which gives you the sensation that your mind has left your body (see pages 213–15 for some simple exercises). If you want to feel more 'in control' you can use more conventional methods such as quiet music, a hot bath or a sentimental film. Whatever you use, you should do it regularly (at least once a day) before too much tension gets stored in your body or your mind is racing so hard that it won't switch off. Get into the habit of always finding five minutes to 'let go' after every highly stressful activity, whether that be an important sales encounter or getting the children off to school.

Finally, don't ever allow yourself to rely on alcohol, pills, cigarettes or even caffeine – if you do, you are just storing up further stress for yourself. Even most tranquillizers prescribed by doctors should be only used in times of severe strain and

> If channelled in the right way, stress can be used to provide the energy for increased performance and self-development.
>
> JANE CRANWELL-WARD

for a very limited amount of time. If you find yourself needing them over a long period then there is almost certainly something wrong with the way you are functioning or your life is being managed. Tackle the root cause before the pill-swallowing habit has a chance to get a hold.

> So much of my public life is about confidence and I'm much less confident when I'm tired. Exhaustion leads to vulnerability.
>
> JULIA NEUBERGER

ARE YOU GETTING ENOUGH REST?

The obvious response to this question is to start counting the hours of sleep that we are getting. Most of us have had the notion firmly imprinted on our minds that we must have a full eight hours, but this is simply not true: the amount recommended will vary from individual to individual. Two of the most energetic Prime Ministers in British history, Winston Churchill and Margaret Thatcher, both survived with merely a few hours per night, even during their most stressful times in office.

If you feel that you are not getting enough rest:

- Establish a strict bedtime hour for the majority of your days per week. Research indicates that our bodies need a regular 'clock' and that the most restful sleep comes in the first few hours. So if you need extra hours in the day, take them early in the morning rather than late at night.
- Prepare your mind and body for a restful sleep by establishing a regular 'winding down' routine before going to bed; children who demand the same nightly rituals know instinctively what they need. (I never used to be able to understand why both my musical daughters demanded an out-of-tune rendering of 'Twinkle, Twinkle, Little Star' each night for so many years!) It doesn't really matter

what you do as long as it doesn't excite your mind or your body too much!

- Keep your nightcaps low in caffeine and alcohol; and for your bedtime snacks keep to easily digestible carbohydrates.
- Check that your bedroom is well ventilated.
- Cat-nap during the day, especially after lunch, which is a low period for most people, so that you do not become over-tired.

> Half an hour's sleep after lunch adds two hours onto my working day.
> WINSTON CHURCHILL

- If you cannot sleep, after 15 minutes or so, get up, make yourself a nourishing drink and snack and do some peaceful activity for a short while. If your head is spinning with worries, sit down and commit these to paper and reassure yourself that you will look at them in the morning.
- Only take sleeping medication for very short periods in times of crisis or extreme disruption of your sleep routines. Like many other women of my generation I spent years poisoning myself with 'non-addictive' sleeping drugs and another few years of restless nights kicking the habit!

Taking Preventative Steps

> In fair weather, prepare for foul.
> PROVERB

Of course, we cannot protect ourselves completely from illness and handicap, but that fact should never stop us from exerting our power over factors which we can control. Preventative health care will never attract vast sums of public money and attention – the pay-offs are too long-term and the 'science' is not exciting and dramatic enough to attract the brilliant. So we must not rely too heavily on 'being looked after' in this area of health care; we must be responsible for taking precautions ourselves.

A positive woman is not a hypochondriac but keeps her head well above the sand. She knows that becoming actively involved in preventative health care is not only sensible, it is psychologically empowering.

As it happens, you have already begun to take a very important step in this field just by reading this book and, I hope, putting into practice some of the ideas which will help you to think, feel and behave less negatively.

SIMPLE PREVENTATIVE MEASURES

Here is a list of preventative measures which are within everyone's control:

- **Keep well informed** – watch the health columns in your newspapers, magazines and the Internet for interesting new research and self-help tips and books. In the wake of a number of important studies which indicated that a positive approach to life strengthens our immune system, a whole new science – psychoneuroimmunology – has begun to flourish. Keep a look-out for more on this subject in particular.
- **Do regular self-checks** – get to know your own warning signals and act promptly when you spot symptoms that need attention. It may be that just altering your lifestyle could be enough. Use your pharmacist for advice – in my experience they are very knowledgeable and helpful. Ring your local health services for advice and leaflets on how to do efficient and thorough checks yourself.
- **Take advantage of screening** – if you are lucky enough to have a 'Well Woman' or similar clinic nearby, then use it. If not, ask your doctor for regular checks on your heart, cholesterol level and blood pressure as well as the obvious cancer screening tests. Does your employer offer any services? If not, ask why not, because many now do! If you have taken any sexual risks you can attend your local hospital's appropriate clinic for a confidential consultation and check.

- **Visit the dentist regularly** – not just to prevent the decay of the teeth themselves for but all the other complaints that infectious mouths can cause or exacerbate. If you fear the dentist (as many more people do than will admit to it), ask your local health or dentistry councils if they know of a practice which uses relaxation, counselling or hypnosis.

- **Make use of self-help organizations and charities** – seek advice and information. Do you have a genetic predisposition towards a particular illness or disease? Don't pretend it will never happen to you; find out if there are any preventative steps you can take. New research is taking place all the time and there may well be some new developments which perhaps weren't available to those who had the condition before.

- **Check your environment** – both at home, at work and in the general community. Do you use more poisonous household cleaning substances than you need to? Are noise levels damaging your ears? Do you campaign for smoke-free public places? Do you use unleaded petrol and encourage others to do so?

- **Check your equipment** – for example, does your furniture and car seat support your back? Is your computer dazzling your eyes? Is your car as safe as it can be? Are the batteries in your smoke detectors fully charged? (Do you have smoke detectors?)

Coping Positively with Illness, Handicap and Ageing

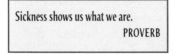

Sickness shows us what we are.

PROVERB

This is certainly an area where one person's tragedy may well be another's opportunity. I can vividly remember my bafflement when, as a naïve young social worker visiting cancer sufferers, I would come out of one house feeling despair and despondency and another feeling uplifted and enriched – even though the social circumstances might be almost identical.

Now, with 25 years of 'worldly wisdom' behind me, I know that the crucial differentiating factors were the sufferer's self-esteem and general attitude to life. If these are positive, we are much more likely to cope efficiently and courageously with any physical difficulty or limitation that may be placed upon us. But there are also some specific steps which you can take which will help you feel more in charge of your life and handicap and may offer considerable practical relief as well.

POSITIVE STRATEGIES

Look for Encouraging Models

> I have found that a sense of humour is a great help. Every now and again I find myself spreadeagled over the bonnet of my car ... it is far better to see a situation as ridiculous rather than upsetting or embarrassing.
>
> ELIZABETH FORSYTHE, a multiple sclerosis sufferer

Although we often knock the media for overdosing us on trouble and tragedy, they do regularly reveal examples of people who cope magnificently with all manner of sickness and handicap. Some stories are, of course, suspiciously sentimental, but there are plenty of others which I certainly find heartening and inspiring. I have included many in my book, *Success from Setbacks*.

> While I'm still comfortably waiting in Death's ante-chamber, I am enjoying myself.
>
> AGATHA CHRISTIE

Join a Self-help or Mutual Aid Group

Being with people who are experiencing the same difficulties provides invaluable support. If there isn't a group in your area, try to start one – contact your local Council for Voluntary Service, or other local voluntary organizations, who will advise you and possibly provide support and administrative help.

> Working to get better treatment and care for people with HIV has given me a powerful motivation in life. I feel I'm contributing something worthwhile ... I'm sure this sense of self-esteem has helped boost my psychological and physical ability to resist the virus.
>
> JONATHAN GRIMSHAW, founder of Body Positive

Become Informed

Send away for free leaflets, order books from the library, contact the relevant charities, demand that your doctor give you full information ... Use assertiveness techniques to help you persist with your enquiries! (See page 96)

Test Out Alternative and Complementary Therapies

– but make sure that you check the credentials and experience of the practitioners first. Books and guides may help (see the Further Reading section) but satisfied customers are always the best test. A confident practitioner will never be short of people willing to talk about their experiences, but don't expect guarantees. Remember that it is not essential that you *like* your therapist or healer, but you do have to be able to *trust* them. If you are starting from a sceptical stance, you will of course need to give them a reasonable chance to earn your trust.

If you prefer to work on your own, try some of the tapes which have recently flooded on to a market hungry for relaxation, meditation, self-hypnosis and creative visualization – all of which should, at the very least, firstly, improve your ability to manage and bear pain and secondly, mobilize any self-healing processes your body can muster. A good way of meeting these kinds of therapists and trying out some of their techniques is to attend a fair or conference on the subject. They are often advertised in the press or local libraries as Mind/Body/ Spirit festivals. (See Part 4 for basic self-help exercises.)

Check Your Entitlement to Financial Help

Don't rely on officials or doctors to inform you of this, because they often don't. Most large towns have voluntary agencies which specialize in welfare rights, however, and some give free legal advice and will represent you at appeals. Check with your local Citizen's Advice Bureau for details. Another idea is to go to the library and look through the *Charities Digest*, because there are many obscure trusts and funds which may be able to give you a grant if you cannot obtain one through the more official channels.

If you have been lucky, or assertive, enough to have consulted a social worker, don't expect them to know all the avenues of help, but do expect them to support your application with a recommendation or confirmation of your need.

Use Advice Columnists

I am very impressed by the quality of information that many of these now give out; they are usually informed of the latest developments and relevant literature, which is more than can be said of many people in the more traditional caring professions! Many 'agony aunts and uncles' now have regular radio and television phone-ins – and several like myself are now offering advice and coaching via the Internet. Don't be overawed by the famous – all those I have met have been very down-to-earth, aware of their own limitations and very caring.

Use the Power of the Media for Campaigning

– but use your assertiveness to make sure you are not abused or patronized by it. Most television and radio stations have special producers who will look after your interests (often in the education or community sections); find out who they are rather than just approaching anyone.

If you are going to be interviewed, prepare your facts and arguments well beforehand. Put these in concise form on two or three index cards so that you can easily refer to them. If possible, rehearse with a friend before you go. Most interviews are now done live (in between the music!) so your 'uhms' and 'ahs' won't be edited out. Don't forget, though, that it is the interviewer who is the professional and it is her or his job to rescue you out of any panic!

Let Yourself Be Cared For

It is often difficult for women to allow themselves to be cared for; many of us feel obliged to keep 'coping' whatever the circumstances. Fortunately, there are many signs that we are becoming a much more caring society. There are so many people who want and need to help others that by asking for aid you'll be doing a favour as well as receiving one. So many people are just waiting for the call and only holding back because they are too frightened of rejection or of hurting someone's feelings.

Don't expect to get all your needs met by one person; some people have wonderfully broad shoulders to cry on, while others are no-nonsense doers and fighters – we usually need both!

Find New Interests and Activities

Don't give yourself the stress of trying to be fitter or younger than you are. This doesn't mean giving up on life and just feeding gracefully on memories of the 'good old days'. Quite the contrary – it means finding things to do which you can enjoy *now* and which will give you reward and satisfaction because you are able to do them well.

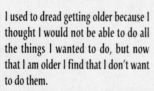

I used to dread getting older because I thought I would not be able to do all the things I wanted to do, but now that I am older I find that I don't want to do them.

NANCY ASTOR, on her eightieth birthday

I find it comforting to think that one of the chief secrets of people who manage to face old age and death positively seems to be that they can look back, not on a charmed life, but on one which they were able to live 'to the full'.

> My life - I had lived in the heights
> and in the depths, in bitter sorrow
> and ecstatic joy, in black despair and
> fervent hope. I had drunk the cup to
> the last drop.
>
> EMMA GOLDMAN

A positive woman respects her body however 'imperfect' or 'old' it may be.

CHAPTER 8

Improving Your Self-presentation

If you are serious about wanting to change yourself and your life, this will probably mean that you will want to equip yourself with a new image as well. I don't think that I have ever known anyone who has not changed their appearance in some way during the course of personal development work. Many negative-thinking people have simply never given enough time and thought to the way they look; they have just drifted into an image and never perhaps had the confidence or motivation to challenge it. Others may have given too much time to their outward appearance – they spend too long worrying about how they are appearing to others at the expense of finding out who they really are and what they really want.

'Changing Your Image'

In this chapter, I do not intend to tell you how you should look, but would like to suggest ways of considering alternative images if you should wish to change your appearance in any way. The changes I see women on personal development courses making are as varied as their personalities. Some start dyeing their hair while others stop dyeing theirs, some start wearing jeans while others start wearing suits, some take off their lipstick while others add lip-liner to theirs. Sometimes they are prompted to change because their new lifestyle requires it, sometimes the change is consciously used as a symbolic reminder of their new attitudes, and sometimes the change happens very subtly and gradually, as they gain more confidence in just being themselves. All are very good reasons!

Based on my experience with working with women on problems of image, I would suggest that there are some basic steps which we can take to help ourselves.

Once again we need to look back as far as our childhood and the messages we received then, both directly and indirectly, because blocks and difficulties are so often rooted there. I hope your memories are not as negative as mine – large, poorly funded children's homes in the 1940s and '50s were not good places to start searching for an individual image!

Explore your memories of your childhood, keeping in mind these basic questions:

- Was I encouraged and supported in the search for my own individual style?
- Was there pressure on me to conform?
- Did I feel the need to rebel?
- What kind of models did I have?

EXPLORE YOUR CONCEPTS

The idea of this step is to help you begin to firm up your own ideas. I have often found that women are held back from making changes because there is an internal war of ideas going on inside their head. It's not surprising, as many of us had confusing personal messages in our childhood and have grown into a world where the public image of women is going through a gigantic transitional period.

Today we are assured that beauty can be as at home in the boardroom as it is in bed. But what is beauty? Is it a scrubbed clean and natural look or is it glamorous and sensual? Is it a 21-inch waist or voluptuous curves? Is it confident elegance or naïve casualness? We are told it can be all of these things, and of course it can – but usually, for some women, some of the time. The key word again seems to be *appropriateness*. Discordancy jars the eye of the beholder. Whatever style is adopted has to suit each individual's personality, mood, body and lifestyle.

Many of us may want to achieve just that – but if we do, we may have to pay a price to make a point. We may not get a job if we don't look the part or not be let in if we wear jeans to the ball ...

The following exercise is designed to help clarify your thoughts about your own style and how that can make you look as beautiful and/or powerful as you want to be.

EXERCISE: MY STYLE

Note your reaction to the following sayings:

- *Beauty is only skin deep.*
- *Beauty is in the eye of the beholder.*
- *Fair face, foul heart.*
- *Appearances are deceptive.*
- *Beauty opens locked doors.*
- *Beauty won't make the pot boil.*
- *Health and wealth create beauty.*
- *Pretty face, poor fate.*

Note your reaction to these quotations by women on the subject of beauty.

- *'Plain women know more about men than beautiful ones do.'* Katharine Hepburn
- *'Glamour is when a man knows a woman is a woman.'* Gina Lollobrigida
- *'Beauty is how you feel inside and it reflects in your eyes. It is not something physical.'* Sophia Loren

- 'A thin woman will get wrinkles sooner than a fat one. So the choice is, "Shall I choose face or figure?" My advice has always been – have a lovely face and sit down.'
Barbara Cartland
- 'Only in romantic novels are the beautiful guaranteed happiness.' Lady Cynthia Asquith
- 'If a guy has some wrinkles it's called character. If a woman has them it's called age.' Cher
- 'There are no ugly women, only lazy ones.'
Helena Rubinstein
- 'When you're 20 and pretty you are rather like Switzerland – beautiful but dull.' Faye Dunaway
- 'It's nothing to be born ugly. Sensibly, the ugly woman comes to terms with her ugliness and exploits it as a grace of nature.' Colette
- 'The concept of beauty for women is based on white male values.' Gloria I. Joseph

Mark the three with which you most identify.

Name six women who *in your opinion* are exceptionally beautiful, women to whom you would give almost 10 out of 10 for self-presentation. (They may or may not be conventionally beautiful.)

List the features of body, clothing, hair, make-up or general appearance that these six women have in common. Are there any major differences?

Complete the following sentence as many times as you can:
Women who want to look good should ...

BREAK YOUR BAD HABITS

Are you sure that you are making rational adult choices about the way you present yourself to the world or has 'habit' got the upper hand? Here are some examples of negative patterns that many women admit to having been slave to. Do you identify with any?

- Trying to 'con' yourself (and sometimes other people) by falsely rationalizing every purchase:
   'I needed a new one anyway (next year!)'
   'It was such a bargain, I thought I would be stupid to miss the opportunity.'
- Not being assertive with sales assistants – feeling overawed or sorry for them.
- Being obsessively tight-fisted – always going for the cheapest, even if that means getting the wrong size or using a whole day's holiday to check the stock of every shop.
- Being too sensible – always taking the 'safest' option; sticking to favourite shops; always under-dressing, but envying the glamour of others.
- Being too extravagant – getting 'carried away'; having a wardrobe full of 'Sunday bests' but not a matching lifestyle; being 'credit card happy'.
- Wanting to be liked – thinking too much of impressing others rather than following your own taste.
- Being lazy – appearing in creased clothes with unpolished shoes, chipped nail varnish ...
- Being a slave to fashion – having to have the latest trend even though it doesn't suit you or you can't afford it.
- Finding yourself 'stuck in a role' – always having to look polished and elegant and not being able to be seen in wellies or without lipstick; sticking to 'the girl-next-door look' when you would like to look outrageous.
- Being obsessive about being overweight – though you may be kilos away from obesity.
- Being obsessive about age – buying anything that will make you look older or younger.
- Being disorganized – never having an outfit prepared and falling into a 'last-minute panic buying syndrome'.

Perhaps you can add to this list – I am sure that I could if I persisted! Hopefully the point has been made: so many of us are not fully in control of our image.

RESEARCH THE ALTERNATIVES

In order to take better charge of your appearance you may need a period in which to experiment. Give yourself a goal, say, to buy a new outfit or change your hairstyle in six months' time. Don't be tempted to go for overnight transformations: your appearance is very important and deserves as much care and attention as other aspects of your self-development.

Use this period of experimentation to gather as much information on alternative ways of dressing as possible:

- buy magazines and cut out interesting features
- closely observe other women and make notes
- buy or borrow books on the subject of self-presentation
- ask for feedback and ideas from trusted friends
- watch free make-up demonstrations and offer to be a guinea-pig
- spring clean your wardrobe and make-up and jewellery drawer and take unwanted items to a charity shop or car boot sale
- watch television programmes on fashion (many of them are on in the day but could be videoed).

When you have spent several months looking around, thinking and experimenting, and you are ready to start building your own new image, remind yourself that the aim is not to choose between certain alternative prepackaged 'looks', but to find a style which assertively celebrates your strengths and builds your confidence. Aim for one which is flexible enough to accommodate the differing roles you have to play but has a recognizable 'core identity'. In other words, one which may have many 'faces' but always allows you to feel and behave like the 'true you', whatever you are wearing or doing.

> The first stage is accepting what you really look like ... concentrate on how you perceive yourself, not what other people think of you ... adapt the look to suit yourself.
>
> BARBARA DALY

The positive woman enjoys being noticed.

CHAPTER 9

Developing
Your Skills
and Knowledge

We have already looked at ways in which you can stimulate and increase the potential of your mind, now we will consider how this positive energy can be channelled into equipping you with extra academic knowledge and practical skills which will enhance your chances of success in whichever field you wish to become proficient.

The Women's Liberation and the feminist movement have achieved remarkable success in drawing everyone's attention to the inequalities of opportunity between men and women and there has been a welcome movement within the educational and training worlds to try to right this wrong. But blanket provisions for extra opportunity are not the only answer: they may help women who are motivated and able to make best use of them, but there are many others who need extra attention and more individual help before they can begin to advance forward.

Having a social work background, and still working voluntarily with many charities, I have met very many women who would never have the energy, let alone the 'know-how', to be able to take advantage of the many new educational and training opportunities that are now available to women. But there are also other reasons for this than simple lack of awareness. Many of the women I see nowadays in my freelance psycho-therapy work are often exceedingly intelligent, informed and probably holding down 'good' jobs, but I have been racking my brains to think of just *one* who has not significantly under-achieved in some way.

Educational Experiences

So what is the difference between these women and the many others who are racing up the career ladder and seizing every training opportunity en route? It is that the former, in spite of sometimes having a 'confident', exterior, are crippled by internal negative feelings about themselves and the world. Almost always, of course, the roots of these feelings can be traced back to very personal childhood experiences at home, at school and in the community. At an early age these women were given the impression that they, either as individuals or as members of the female sex, were not destined for the heights of educational glory!

In contrast, many successful women talk of how, for sometimes very personal reasons, their parents *expected* them to achieve academically and did not allow gender prejudice to infiltrate their home:

One of the things that I am extremely grateful for is that neither parent ever saw my life in terms of marriage and babies and the female lot. Both of them regarded education as the top priority of my life and they were gender-blind.

ESTHER RANTZEN

In the family there was the aspiration for us to succeed educationally and the sharing out of domestic tasks, looking after the baby, doing the washing up, trying to get to school was very equal.

CLARE SHORT

> My parents were highly motivated to have us educated ... it was simply that we should not be denied what they had been denied ... my father would have preferred sons ... we were talked to as though we had the minds of boys.
>
> JOAN RUDDOCK

SCHOOL DAYS

When I am working with clients, the subject of school comes up very frequently. Very often it holds many memories of unfair or disillusioned teachers, boring and inappropriate lessons or competitive, cruel, teasing peers. All such experiences can permanently taint learning with negativity. In contrast, look at Anita Roddick's memories and their lasting effect:

> I had two mentors who were teachers. To this day I am only trying to please them ... they made me feel so special ... and when you are told that you are going to be special often enough you wear that specialness around you like a cloak.
>
> ANITA RODDICK

So the first step you should take is to understand how you may be sabotaging your own chances by not taking advantage of the educational and training opportunities that there are around today. You should become aware of any negative experiences that may have resulted in a negative attitude towards learning. This will help you to feel that you *deserve extra* help and stimulation in order to make up for any lost time!

EXERCISE: MY EDUCATION

Ask yourself if you have been held back by any of the following kinds of influences:

- *mother's or father's negative attitude and/or example*
- *living in the shadow of clever brothers/sister/cousins, etc.*
- *lack of stimulation – books, newspapers, educational outings, musical instruments*
- *inept, cruel or indifferent teachers*
- *under-resourced school (not enough art material, no computers, a skeleton library with old-fashioned books, no careers counselling)*
- *under-ambitious school ('We never manage to get anyone to the best universities ...')*
- *over-ambitious school ('If you don't get to university, what's the point?')*
- *inappropriate lessons and teaching methods which didn't encourage you to develop your interests and skills (e.g. cookery for the girls and woodwork for the boys; geography without the field projects; over or underemphasis on sport or academic learning)*
- *unfortunate critical examination result (failing 11 plus or entrance scholarship)*
- *bullying, over-competitive or jealous peers*
- *racism*
- *too frequent change of schools*
- *distracting and energy-sapping traumas during school life (family disharmony, bereavements, war, disasters)*
- *being held back through illness and never getting a chance to catch up*

Educational Opportunities

The next step is to think of the kind of education and training which would have helped you to realize your full potential and find out whether you can get any of that for yourself now, as an adult. Many of my clients have been helped to do this by taking time to think about their interests and aptitudes as far back as their first school days – i.e. before the negative influences began to take their toll. Many have surprised themselves by remembering how excited they were about maths or sport or art – or proudly recalled how good their essays used to be, how well they played the violin or how good they were at organizing everyone. It was very rewarding for me to then see them find a way of stimulating these 'lost' or neglected aptitudes and, as a result, find many new opportunities.

WAYS FORWARD

Let's look at some additional steps you can take if you would like to develop your knowledge and skills.

Career and Educational Counselling and Advice

This should be available free from your local authority. Contact your own adult education office for details. The service in some areas is more sophisticated than in others and you may feel the need to supplement this with sessions from an independent counsellor or psychologist (usually advertised in the press but your education office or Citizen's Advice Bureau might be able to help with contacts.) Alternatively you can borrow or buy many books which will not only give you information about all the courses available but explain the meanings of the different qualifications. Many of these also contain exercises and tests to enable you to find out more about your aptitudes. (See the Further Reading section.)

Experiment with Adult Education Classes

Try different short courses to see if you have the 'taste' for certain subjects. Don't rely on the programme offering you just what you need – if there isn't the course that you would like, ask the adult education office to put one on – they will respond positively if there is sufficient demand (ask your friends or colleagues if they are interested.)

Join a Pre-higher Education Course

Some of these are courses especially designed for women who want to get back to studying but are not quite sure where to start. They are often labelled 'Return to Study', 'Fresh Start' or 'Fresh Horizons'. Some are held in the evening and some during the day. Most will have creche facilities and they are usually very cheap.

Find the Money

With all the cutbacks in education this is becoming an increasing problem, but don't let lack of resources hold you back until you are sure you have exhausted all the possibilities.

- Local citizen's advice or adult education offices will give you some initial information about where to go to find out if you are eligible for **statutory grants**, and my experience is that often the quickest and most pleasant way of finding out about the possibilities is to contact the leader, or one of the tutors, on the course you want to go on. They are usually motivated to help because they want you to do the course (yes, most do!) and they have the experience of other students to draw on.
- Ask about the possibility of **subsidies and bursaries** – don't ever rely on people to tell you about these often closely guarded 'secrets' automatically.
- Try approaching your **local Equal Opportunities department** for help and advice – especially if you have an additional 'handicap' (i.e. other than being female!) They have knowledge of **grants** and also of sympathetic employers who may be able to give you in-service training.
- Contact your **Department of Employment**, particularly if you have been unemployed for a long time, because there

are many excellent **re-training courses** available free of charge!

- Dig out a digest on local and national charities from the library and work your way through it. Type a well-argued 'begging letter' and send it to as many **charities and trusts** as you can. I know someone who has funded themselves through a whole three-year degree course by getting literally hundreds of small grants. (This was someone who had already had their grant quota from the state for a degree course which turned out to be a terrible mistake.)

- If you are working towards a professional qualification, contact the **appropriate associations** and bodies, as sometimes they give grants as well as advice.

- You could also try your employer, but make sure that you couch your request in terms which she or he will appreciate. This usually means spelling the potential economic benefit to the company or organization of your studies! I have known many people be very surprised with the results of doing just this.

- Alternatively you could suggest that the course you want to do is arranged as an **in-house training event** which could benefit others as well. I know that many training officers respond very favourably to such requests. Whatever you do, don't waste time waiting to be sent on a course!

- Finally, approach your bank manager or any other source of **loans** (maybe a rich relative!) If you can argue that doing a course is an investment in your career potential then many will be forthcoming with the money. This is the way that I have funded almost all the courses I have done in my adult life and I can certainly vouch for the rewards of taking this risk.

Women's educational goals have, of course, been transformed beyond recognition, this century:

> The three great stumbling blocks in a girl's education, she says are 'hommard a la Americaine', a boiled egg and asparagus.
>
> COLETTE

but we do still have major stumbling blocks. The three main ones confronting today's women are prejudice, confidence and money. Looking on the positive side, however, I would say that at least they do present a more interesting challenge than boiled eggs!

The positive woman is proud to be an eternal student.

THREE

Getting

into

Action

CHAPTER 10

Revitalizing Personal Relationships

> Most pathfinders carry a little secret: they are not entirely alone. Someone else takes their dreams and illusions, their good times and bad times, their triumphs and defeats, almost as seriously as they themselves do.
>
> GAIL SHEEHY

Traditionally, personal relationships have been the most important area in women's lives. Now that we have many more opportunities to gain satisfaction and earn respect and admiration, our work and leisure pursuits may have become equally, if not sometimes more important to many of us. But however high or low our relationships may rank in our priority stakes, they very rarely get the critical appraisals they deserve. All too often they are just taken for granted or are allowed to muddle along. How often we hear:

'It's just my luck to have found someone like him.'
'I've been blessed with two wonderful children.'
'Fortunately, I have a really good supportive Mum.'
'They are a pair of star-crossed lovers.'
'You are my destiny ... we were made for each other.'

➤

'There's always a black sheep in every family.'
'Marriages are made in heaven.'

Would you ever catch efficient managers talking like this about their staff, or see captains of Olympic teams letting fate pick the side? Of course not, because they can probably take the credit for selecting the appropriate people and, even if they have 'inherited' the members of their team, they take responsibility for fostering and maintaining good working relationships. But even 'wonder managers' may have a very different attitude to their personal lives, feeling just as power-less and fatalistic as anyone else. I think that there are several important factors which contribute towards forming these kinds of attitudes:

1. As our first – and most influential – experience of personal relationships was when we were children (when we were indeed powerless), at some deep, pervasive level we associate family and other similar close relationships with feelings of helplessness and dependency.
2. As women are only just beginning to emerge from centuries of economic and social dependence on the men with whom they were personally involved, the very idea of assuming overt power in this area of their lives is still both unfamiliar and scary.
3. It is only in the last half of this century that the arts and sciences of psychology and therapy have given us the insight and skills to make changes in our relationships. Up until recently the alternatives (for those who could afford the choice) were 'love them or leave them'.

As emancipated adult women, however, we can and should take responsibility for the quality of our personal relation-ships. Research indicates that if these are satisfying and secure, we will feel happier, healthier, more self-confident and more able to withstand stress and take risks. How can any positive woman do without them!

So use this section to help you check out whether you have the kind of relationships you want and deserve, and to get ideas on how you can take more effective control of them.

Marriage and Other Intimate Partnerships

> Liberation is having the opportunity to do your own thing.
> Marriage enabled me to do it more confidently, more successfully.
> MARY STOTT

Most women will experience intimate partnerships with a man but there are growing numbers of women who are choosing to develop them with other women. So even though the following questions and points are based largely on my own personal and professional experience of marriage, I hope that some of them will be relevant to anyone who is closely involved in any intimate love relationship with another adult.

ARE YOUR OBJECTIVES AND DREAMS REALISTIC?

The first point to consider is whether you and your partner both share the same expectations and hopes of what your partnership is all about. It is unlikely that you do, because there are so many individual variations on this particular theme. You may appear to do so in the early days of your relationship, when no doubt you will have talked frequently about your ideas and values, and (unless your partnership is one of 'convenience') you are unlikely to have settled for someone with very different dreams to your own. But unfortunately those early days are not always the best times to be negotiating about the objectives and goals of our relationships because we are so starry-eyed and romantic that our conscious outlook will be heavily influenced by the current fashionable models of 'ideal' relationships in our particular culture.

Of course, after some time of being or living together, many couples find that their actual behaviour and feelings do not match the dream.

> Marrying a man is like buying something you have been admiring for a long time in a shop window. You may love it when you get it home, but it doesn't always go with everything else in the house.
>
> JEAN KERR

This discrepancy is largely because our subconscious selves start to assert their own values and needs. In earlier chapters we have already discussed how these are heavily influenced by our experiences in childhood. As soon as intimacy begins to develop we start to feel and respond according to the way we were 'programmed' in our most influential and powerful close relationships – which are usually with our parents. So the seeds of almost inevitable internal conflict are sown, because even if you came from the happiest of homes, no doubt you would still prefer your partnership to be based on *your* ideals and needs rather than those of a previous generation. But the *real* problems occur when many of the original patterns and models were negative, because they will leave a legacy of destructive attitudes and behaviour patterns.

The first step towards setting realistic goals and objectives for your relationship is to *accept* that you might try to make your relationship mirror that of your parents: that you might behave like a replica of your mother and he like his father. Take an objective look at both your original family experiences and be forewarned!

Of course, our family background is not the only influence our 'auto-pilot' will bring to bear on our partnership. There are many others which will also need considering. But, as we have noted many times already, the positive woman does not *have* to be a slave to the past – she can use *insight* and *constructive mutual feedback* to help break negative habits.

EXERCISE: SUBCONSCIOUS INFLUENCES ON MY RELATIONSHIP

This exercise is one which you could do with your partner, but if this is not possible, make sure that on completing it, you do at the very least discuss your thoughts on the subject together. Remember that your 'influences' can infiltrate your relationship either as rightful 'shoulds' or as rebellious 'should nots'.

Complete these sentences, as many times as you can, using the examples given as a guide.

As a result of my family background, my 'auto-pilot' is likely to think that:

– marriage (or a similar close partnership) is ...
  for life
  likely to end in divorce
  unhappy
– couples ...
  should always be faithful
  cannot ever really trust each other
– a husband will ...
  protect the woman
  abuse the woman
  be unfaithful
– a wife should ...
  be the peacemaker
  stay at home
  look beautiful
– sex is ...
  strictly for the bedroom
  an uncontrollable urge
  something a woman does to keep her man
  for procreation
  only permissible between men and women

Complete similar sentences in relation to your partner's background.

Examine other very important unconscious influences on your relationship. What expectations do you both bring into the partnership? You might like to consider:
- *your gender conditioning*
- *your class conditioning*
- *your religious beliefs*
- *any 'unfinished business' from previous relationships*
- *the example of your circle of friends or colleagues*

HAVE YOU NEGOTIATED CLEAR GROUND RULES?

Once you have done this exercise and had a discussion with your partner, you can begin to start thinking about having a realistic contract with each other which is based on mutual understanding of each other's background and perception of partnerships. You can begin to think about the 'rules' you may want to try to base the relationship on. These will of course vary enormously from couple to couple, but it may help to find your own if you at least know what guidelines other people have found useful. The following are some basic principles which research has indicated that successful and happy marriages are based upon. Use it as a checklist.

1. Mutual trust.
2. Respect for each other's privacy.
3. Emotional support.
4. Fidelity.
5. Equitable sharing of household expenses and chores.
6. Looking after each other in times of illness and misfortune.
7. Showing interest in each other's activities.
8. Allowing each other to have some independence.
9. Being clear about time-keeping.
10. Keeping confidences.
11. Disclosing personal feelings about each other.
12. Talking about problems concerning the relationship.
13. Never being violent.
14. Agreeing before major expenditure of joint finances.

➤

IS THERE ENOUGH ROMANCE AND CELEBRATION IN THE RELATIONSHIP?

> Pride - that's a luxury a woman in love can't afford.
>
> CLARE BOOTHE LUCE

This is an area where women have traditionally taken the lead from men even though we have, reputedly, the more romantic needs! How many of us still expect to receive bouquets, wait for the candle-lit dinner to be booked and then listen patiently for the 'sweet nothings' to be whispered in our ears? I can understand my generation playing this courtship game (because I am so keen to absolve myself) but I was surprised to hear that it is still very much around in the partnerships of younger generations. The major share of the Valentine market is still male and when I was recently interviewing young men in their teens and twenties, they all told me that girls still expected to be courted and romantically wooed. They expressed resentment that their gestures were not reciprocated: 'They want equality but ...'

Many modern women have become understandably cynical about romance because they are all too aware of the damage the Prince Charming myth can do to their struggle for equality and justice. Romance has been a traditional tool for luring women into compliance with the general social injustices of our patriarchal society and with abusive sexist practices within personal relationships. Many of us are still haunted by uncomfortable memories of being seduced by 'charming' fathers, boyfriends or colleagues and bosses into 'forgiving the unforgivable', only to find ourselves deceived, exploited or abused yet again. We may have therefore learned to mistrust proclamations and promises which are accompanied by iced champagne, continental chocolates and red roses. But all intimate relationships nevertheless do need to be regularly fed with some kind of positive nourishment, so it is important to find some mutually acceptable way of doing this.

If you do not like the traditional symbols of romance, make sure that you have alternative ways of expressing your continuing love, appreciation and commitment. Don't rely too heavily on the spontaneity which is often enough in those early 'heady' days – with the passage of time it is so easy to drift into taking each other for granted, even in the most loving and caring of relationships. 'I didn't know you still cared' or 'If only you had told me you loved me before it was too late' are typical of the cries I have heard many people make to partners who are begging them not resort to divorce.

IS YOUR RELATIONSHIP GETTING ITS FAIR SHARE OF POSITIVE NOURISHMENT?

EXERCISE: NOURISHING LOVE

Ask yourself:

- *Do you compliment each other frequently?*
- *Do you continue to specify why you love each other?*
- *How many celebrations of successes have you had this year?*
- *Do you ever give surprise presents?*
- *Are your 'special days' special enough?*
- *Are you giving yourself enough time just to be alone together?*
- *How often do you use cuddles and hugs to express love rather than just to stimulate each other sexually?*

Show your answers to your partner; talk and make your resolutions!

DO YOU CARE ENOUGH ABOUT YOURSELF IN THE RELATIONSHIP?

In our culture there are so many direct and indirect messages which suggest that the woman's role in intimate relationships with men is that of nurturing partner, that often in spite of their conscious efforts to the contrary women still do end up giving their own needs low priority. It is not surprising that Robin Norwood's book *Women Who Love Too Much* or Colette Dowling's *The Cinderella Complex* should have reached the best-seller list.

Look at the following list. Do you find yourself:

- biting your tongue for peace's sake if you are doing more than your fair share of housework, in spite of the fact that you are permanently exhausted
- dressing to suit him rather than wearing what you feel comfortable and at home in
- watching his favourite television programmes rather than your own
- going to social or sports events which bore you silly
- making love more or less often than you wish or participating in sexual games which either bore or disgust you
- feeling sorry for him when he looks so hurt after your justified criticism
- making excuses for him because he has forgotten your birthday or anniversary
- moving from a much loved house, community or job to further his career.

On their own many of these 'loving' gestures may be insignificant, but if many are repeated often enough they will gradually wear down your self-esteem and make it even more difficult for you to assert your own needs and wants. If you found yourself identifying with any of the above, talk to your partner. Perhaps he hasn't even noticed what is happening – very many men, on the break-up of their relationships, express genuine surprise to me that their wives feel so 'hard-done-by'. Don't forget that however much of a 'New Man' your partner is, he will have been affected to some degree by the masculine conditioning which will have brought him up to take for granted this kind of sacrificial care and attention from women.

> Recovery begins when we become willing to channel the energy and effort that we formerly spent on trying to bring about change in someone else into instead changing ourselves. Our initial steps may not come very quickly or easily, and they may at first be very small, but we must learn to respect their importance.
>
> ROBIN NORWOOD

DO YOU ASK FOR WHAT YOU WANT IN AN ASSERTIVE MANNER?

> Men and women who are understood by those they love achieve this by communicating who they are. They do not passively await a magical kind of intuition from their beloved.
>
> Drs CONNELL and KINDER

Women have been conditioned, generally speaking, to get what they want from men using *passive* tactics. We have been fed with a variety of messages on the themes of:

'The way to a man's heart is through his stomach.'
'The art of getting what you want from a man is to make him think that it was his idea.'
' Ask him in bed.'
'Flattery will get you everywhere with a man.'

So remember your assertive skills. (You may like to check the section on Broken Record, p. 93). Don't expect his love to read your mind.

When making requests be:

- **Positive** – let it be known that you are optimistic about the outcome. (Don't start with 'You're probably going to bite my head off ...')
- **Direct** – give up waiting for the hint to sink in!
- **Concise** – don't provide lectures and unnecessary justifications.
- **Realistic** – don't expect him to think the same way you do or change his habits overnight.

- **Persistent** – even though this may be interpreted as nagging!

IS YOUR SEXUAL RELATIONSHIP GOOD ENOUGH?

> When we look at the subject of sex and assertiveness, we know it is explosive and that we need to go carefully but that does not alter the fact that we still need to go.
>
> ANN DICKSON

Far too many women still put up with frustrating and frankly boring sex lives. And far too many women still 'allow' things to happen in bed which make them feel uncomfortable and even degraded.

All these women are damaging their self-esteem and missing out on an aspect of life which could give them extra warmth, fun and energy. Many may have calculated that the pluses in their relationship make this 'sacrifice' worthwhile, but many others simply have not tried to alter their sexual lives in an assertive manner. They often feel too embarrassed to even bring the subject up. Some are frightened of losing their relationship if they do, while others are scared of hurting the other person if they are critical and, of course, being women, many feel that it must be *their* fault anyway!

If your sex life isn't fulfilling, before talking to your partner you could prepare yourself by:

- helping to beat any feelings of ignorance and embarrassment by buying or borrowing relevant books. Don't be shy about getting hold of these – they are usually found in the medical section and there are many excellent ones now on the market.
- re-awakening your body to safe sensual pleasure by having a massage, if you are feeling 'switched off'
- masturbating, if you are overly tense and frustrated
- talking to a trusted female friend about your difficulty
- booking an appointment with a counsellor – many now have special training in sexual problems and would be happy to have an initial counselling session with just one partner.

When you feel ready, have a discussion with your partner, but make sure that the time and place is appropriate. Choose a place where you can both feel private and relaxed, and don't forget to start with a positive and optimistic tone. Remind yourself that only a very tiny proportion of sexual difficulties are due to 'mechanical' problems and that it's most likely to be a psychological block that is getting in the way. Avoid taking or giving blame – the vast majority of problems are caused by a 'fault' in the relationship, so both of you have some responsibility for making changes.

If your self-help strategies don't work, ask your doctor to refer you to a sex therapist or counsellor.

DO YOU ARGUE ENOUGH?

> Never go to bed mad. Stay up and fight.
> PHYLLIS DILLER

Obviously I am not advocating a life of constant rows and quarrels, but very few intimate relationships can grow and prosper without regular arguments to settle differences and the occasional row to clear the air.

There may be several reasons why your partnership is not volatile enough. Firstly, you may still be too 'nice'. We have already noted how female conditioning makes it difficult for many women to express feelings of frustration and anger, and I hope you are now convinced of the need to learn to handle this feeling both in yourselves and others.

Secondly, your relationship may be too insecure and either you or your partner – or both – may be trying to protect the fragile 'status quo' by sitting on any disagreements.

Thirdly, you may not care enough to bother quarrelling:

> Boredom leads to indifference, which is probably one of the worst human feelings there is and, incidentally one of the real causes of divorce ... fighting is better than being bored.
> VIRGINIA SATIR

Fourthly, you may be living in fear of violence.

None of these reasons should be good enough for a woman who wants to live her life to the full, so if you find your partnership wanting, act positively to either revive it – or end it.

ARE YOU PREPARED FOR THE POSSIBILITY OF DIVORCE OR SEPARATION?

You may think that this is a strange question but remember that positive women are contingency planners – they do not deny problems or the possibility of misfortune, but make sure that they are prepared for the worst, even though they hope for the best (see page 90). Now most women are sensible enough to make some preparation for the possibility of premature widowhood, but few want to face the increasing likelihood of divorce or separation. Yet no one can count anymore on 'happily ever after' relationships – serial marriage may well be more the norm for very many of us.

As someone who was once taken totally by surprise by the sudden breakdown of a seemingly happy marriage, I am convinced that women, and women with children in particular, need to confront and prepare for these possibilities. My experience of encouraging people to do just this has led me to believe that the exercise can actually have a positive and healing effect on insecure relationships. If you are convinced that you will survive a break-up, this gives you a sense of power which will assist you in attempts to right the wrongs in your relationship.

Unless you feel divorce or separation is highly imminent, your preparation does not need to be detailed and thorough but, at the very least, you could think through the various options and possible strategies for coping.

EXERCISE: SURVIVING SEPARATION

Ask yourself the following questions:

- *Who can I turn to for support? Have I enough friends who wouldn't feel torn between us? Would my family support me or would they disapprove?*
- *What other strategies have I for looking after myself through what would be stressful and despairing times?*
- *How would I survive financially? Do I need my own resources to fall back on? What about my pension rights? Would I be able to get back on the career ladder very easily?*
- *Where would I live? Is the house or flat in joint names? Is there somewhere where I could go for temporary shelter, if necessary?*
- *If a crisis occurred (such as the uncovering of an affair) would we try to hide everything from the children or do we believe in keeping them informed? How would we ensure that they were not used as weapons between us?*
- *Do I know my legal rights and have I access to a good solicitor?*

> Marriage is lovely when it works, but if it does not, should one condemn oneself?
>
> BUCHI EMECHETA

> Knowing how few people enjoy that kind of security and knowledge of love, I marvel at the childhood that I once took for granted.
>
> MONICA DICKENS

Children

The whole issue of children is of vital concern because parents who think and act negatively can, and do, people our politically and ecologically fragile world with at best dithering, apathetic martyrs and at worst bitter, cynical egocentrics. This is a belief which, thank goodness, is no longer just held by psychologists and 'do-gooders' but has almost become a universal truth. Day after day it seems to be confirmed by media biographies which reveal the negative parenting of our waifs and strays, as well our murderers and dictators. It is further confirmed by the growing demand for advice and help from concerned women who are frightened that they are making, or in danger of making, irreversible mistakes.

This is perhaps especially so for those of us whose parenting task is further complicated because we do not have straightforward nuclear family arrangements. For several years I was a single parent, and no sooner had I adjusted to the particular problems of that parenting challenge, than I chose to take on the added responsibility of being a step-mother and helping my children adjust to a new step-father! I wonder what trials are in store for me as a grandparent!

In this section I will discuss some of the major issues which I, and other parents with whom I have worked, have considered important to address, and work on, if we wish our parenting to be a positive experience for both ourselves and our children.

TO HAVE OR HAVE NOT

The first question any woman today must ask herself is: 'Do I actually *want* children?' This is too big a question to be answered with a simple 'yes' or 'no' gut response. Many women feel that the advancement of science and women's liberation have given us a welcome choice but an unwelcome responsibility. We carry the burden of making a difficult decision. Assuming that you are empowered enough to have a good deal of control over your feelings and lifestyle, this will mean seriously confronting, and accepting, who you actually are and what you actually believe in. Most of us know that we can no longer look to our 'circumstances' for the answers, as we have far more control over them than ever before. We know that:

- if we have a lover we can use contraception
- if we have a career we can arrange child-minding (or find a 'house husband'!)
- if we have no partner we can join a dating agency or even try artificial insemination

- if we are infertile, we can adopt or foster
- if we have an 'accident' we can use the Morning After pill or even have an abortion
- if we are over 30 we can have some tests
- if we feel that we are too neurotic we can get therapy
- if we have had no useful models to show us how, we can read books and join parenting classes
- if we have an unwilling partner we can get divorced.

The buck now stops with us! But many women find this too hard a fact to swallow and so they seek the support and guidance of therapists. Others find it so hard that they deny even to themselves that it is a problem; they bring all manner of complaints to the consulting room, but it is only after months of self-exploration that they discover that this is indeed a big issue for them. My own observation is that this is happening increasingly frequently to professional women in their mid-to-late thirties who, consciously or unconsciously, realize that nature will soon rob them of one option.

If a decision is made to have a child, the next question facing a woman is when. Should they plan their childbearing at the start of a career or the end of a career, or should babies and work just integrate together at any time?

Of course there are no easy answers to any of these questions and certainly I would not venture to give even the most general guidelines, but I would make a strong plea for doing some *positive* decision-making rather than procrastinating or waiting for fate or an upsurge of maternal instinct to show you the direction. I have heard so many women say 'I wish I had thought about this sooner.' You could start by using the strategies described in Chapter 4 or arrange a talk with an unbiased friend or counsellor.

POSITIVE PARENTING

I wonder, if I could have foreseen all the parenting blunders I have made, whether I would still have taken the risk? I hope so, because the mothering of my two daughters has been the most exciting and rewarding experience of my whole life. Although I adored both my children from the first moment I saw them, any natural mothering instincts I may have had in my genes were obscured at first by a thick fog of anxiety and terror. Of course it didn't help that I had spent my own childhood being looked after by substitute parents who seemed more interested in the cleanliness and godliness of their institutions than in me. Nor that my professional training and experience had given me an insight into all the dreadful consequences of bad parenting. But I soon found out that I was not alone in my apprehension. A whole generation of women seemed to be struggling to 'get it right'. The great advances taking place in the fields of psychology and child development were receiving media coverage, and we were overawed by our responsibility and the conflicting theories which were presented to us.

Thank goodness the following generations seem generally to be feeling more confident and self-assured and therefore more able to trust their own instincts. But there is still a sizable proportion of women who are not so lucky and are looking for guidance because they are aware that their relationship with their children is not quite 'good enough'. If you are one of these, use the following section as a checklist and food for thought, but don't expect it to be the miracle Bible that every self-doubting parent prays for! Each day I learn something new about being a mother, either from my children, my clients or my books; I find the knowledge both fascinating and helpful, but have long since given up the search for complete enlightenment.

Blocks to Positive Parenting

The following are some of the major difficulties that I have noticed preventing women being the kind of mothers they would like to be.

Unhealed Hurt from Our Own Childhood

We have already considered how this can generally affect our ability to think, act and feel positively, but in our roles as parents it can be especially restricting. Just being with our children in everyday situations can stir up the memory bank of the subconscious and can open up wounds without our even realizing that it is happening. Very few parents would knowingly set about holding their children back or abusing them to make up for their own hurt, but many do exactly that without knowing it. In an attempt to 'do her best' for her children a mother may end up:

- over-indulging her children (because her own mother never had enough time for her)
- being over-ambitious for her children (because her parents never encouraged her academic progress)
- never standing up for herself and cutting arguments too short (because her own family life was so turbulent)
- making her children grow up too quickly (because her mother was so clingy)
- putting down her son's 'masculine' interests (because her own father was so sexist)
- moving house continually (because her parents were so parochial and never encouraged her adventurousness)
- over-disciplining (because her parents told her that it 'did her good' and she believed them as it was the only way she could make sense of the injustice)
- not letting her daughter get close to her father (because her own father abused her)
- not being positive and encouraging enough about school (because her own school-days were so unhappy).

Being aware of these hurts and working on healing them is especially important if you want to ensure that they won't also damage your children.

Lack of Self-love

> My mother was a frustrated woman and she put a lot of ambition into making us ambitious. She herself hadn't found an outlet for her undeniable intelligence ... I think I would have been happier if I had had a slightly more normal home life.
>
> MARGARET DRABBLE

Without this it is very difficult to truly love anyone else. Unfortunately self-love is often confused with selfishness, which had been considered totally unacceptable by generations of mothers. Psychoanalyst Erich Fromm, in his classic study *The Art of Loving*, argues that selfishness and self-love are far from being identical; they are in fact opposites. Selfish people hate themselves as well as being incapable of loving others. Certainly my experience of working with hundreds of adults who have been damaged by 'martyr mothers' supports the theory that self-love is an all important prerequisite for positive parenting. Children are proud of mothers who love themselves enough to want to make something of their own lives, and will want to follow their example.

> My mother is very important to me. She broke the rules, she did things in her life that I am immensely proud of.
>
> ANITA RODDICK

Mothers who are obsessively 'unselfish' block their children by:

– being too hard an act to follow, and so making the child always feel 'guilty' when rightfully asserting themselves or giving themselves pleasure
- making a child feel reluctant to separate because they know that without them their mother's life will be empty and purposeless
- leaving them without adequate self-protective skills; they can never criticize and use their anger because mother never showed them how to, and also seemed to 'fall apart' if they tried to experiment with standing up for themselves

– being sick and unhappy, and therefore giving a child a negative view of the adult world.

> It was my daughter who often seemed most meaningful in my struggle for my lost self. She was my little Echo, my 'mirror' the answer to a mother's dreams ... Gabrielle's achievements were something I used to boost my own self-esteem: her achievements became my achievements.
>
> COLETTE DOWLING

Trying Too Hard

Attempts to be the perfect parent and create the ideal happy family can cripple our children because it can cripple our own spontaneity and creativity. We see so many models of 'perfection' in the media that we can constantly find ourselves wanting.

> Perfection is not within the grasp of ordinary human beings. Efforts to attain it typically interfere with that lenient response to imperfections of others, including those of one's child, which alone make good human relations impossible.
>
> BRUNO BETTELHEIM

Nancy Friday in *My Mother, Myself* writes movingly of a fantasy scene with her mother which, if it had taken place, might have transformed their relationship. She imagines that her mother calls her into her room and says, 'Nancy, you know I am not very good at this mothering business. You're a lovely child, the fault is not with you. But motherhood does not come easily to me. So when I do not seem like other people's mothers, try to understand that it isn't because I don't love you. I do. But I am confused myself.'

Like so many of my clients (and myself) Nancy Friday was not looking for a perfect mother, but rather one who simply assertively admitted her mistakes and inadequacies and did not make her feel intrinsically a failure because she could not be the perfect product one expects from perfect mothering!

Accepting that you cannot be the perfect mother makes it easier for children to get important parenting 'goodies' from other caring adults – for example their father, grandparents, child-minders and youth leaders. When you are aiming for perfection, it is difficult to trust anyone else to be 'in on the act'. As roles in the family are changing and women have other interests and duties apart from motherhood, shared parenting is becoming more essential.

In addition an imperfect but 'good enough' mother can accept that the 'happy family' will not always be harmonious if individuality is allowed to flourish, and therefore will encourage an atmosphere where negative feelings and ambivalent attitudes, as well as love and caring, can be healthily expressed. Children will then have an authentic atmosphere where they can feel free to explore different aspects of themselves.

AIDS TO BUILDING CONFIDENCE AND POSITIVE ATTITUDES IN CHILDREN

Assuming that we ourselves are exemplary models of the above (!), what else can we do to actively foster these qualities in our children? The following is a list which I have compiled with the help of many clients who have learned much by being both children of 'not good enough' parents and by being imperfect examples themselves.

Provide Basic Shelter and Security

This involves keeping your important relationships, your own health and your bank balance in as healthy condition as possible, so that the family is not lurching from crisis to crisis all the time. If security does get shattered occasionally, it means assuring the children that stability *will* return; and demonstrating how it can be rebuilt on a whole variety of foundations.

Convey Unconditional Admiration

It's not enough to love our children: we have to communicate our feelings in a way that a child understands best. Some of these are cuddles and hugs, a genuine willingness to share time with them, and showing interest in activities and achievements which do not seem particularly exciting to us. Our love and admiration must be seen to be without strings and must embrace the whole of our children's personalities. We must not admire them most when they are acting in our image or fulfilling our dreams.

My mother always said, you can be anything you want in the world, you just have to 'think positive'; any goal you want you can have if you believe in yourself.

JERRY HALL

My mother believed in me strongly ... if you grow up with that feeling it gives you great strength. Somehow I took it for granted that I would be able to do certain things.

CLAIRE TOMALIN

My mother gave me the sense of myself that says, 'No-one is going to grind you down.'

CLEO LAINE

Teach Communication Skills

Teach your children how to be direct, how to negotiate, how to make small talk, how to express their feelings and how to be appropriately assertive, passive or aggressive. My book *Confident Children* contains many tips on how you can do this.

Develop Their Independence Gradually

Be sensitive and respectful of their pace and allow them to be dependent as long as they to need to be.

Also, of course, demonstrate to them that you can survive very well without them when they begin to take their inevitable steps away from you!

> A child who has been breastfed for nine months and no longer wants to drink from the breast does not have to be taught to give it up. And a child that has been allowed to be egotistic, greedy and asocial long enough will develop spontaneous pleasure in sharing and giving.
>
> ALICE MILLER

Encourage Self-discipline and Self-assessment

It is part of our duty as parents to give our children a sense of right and wrong. But we need to do more than just preach morality to them: we need to have a clear set of values which is consistently reflected in a code of behaviour which we firmly insist on being respected.

While children are still too young to be able to take full responsibility for themselves, we may need to use disciplinary measures to enforce this code of behaviour, but as soon as they are old enough to understand, we should help them to see the rationale behind our values and 'rules'. This means answering their tedious 'Why do I have to ...' questions with more reasoning than 'Because I told you to.' It involves encouraging them to discuss and argue their 'case' with logic and reason, to develop empathy by getting into your 'shoes' or the 'shoes' of the person whom they may be hurting or offending and understand the ultimate consequences of their 'bad' behaviour. It also involves helping them to be aware of the rewards they can expect if they do comply with your wishes or the rules of their school or the laws of society, so that they will develop self-discipline because they want to do what is right. As they get older we should ask them to make judgements about their own behaviour based on their own goals, abilities and values and discourage continual comparison with other people's behaviour or successes and failures.

Challenge Sexual Stereotypes

Value and encourage the expression of the 'feminine' and 'masculine' side of all children, regardless of their gender, but be sensitive to their ambivalent feelings when they come under the influence of cultural pressure from a society which still sells the Barbie Doll and Action Man myths.

Girls need to learn to value their warm, nurturing qualities but at the same time be taught the assertive skill of saying 'no' when they need space for themselves or they are being exploited. They need to have their intuitive powers and their sensitivity to feelings valued but also be helped to develop the left-brained skills which will enable them to compete effectively in our computer age. They should also be taught to appreciate and develop their adaptability and flexibility without compromising their basic sense of their own identity and their own values.

Boys, on the other hand, need help with learning to express their feelings openly without going 'over the top' so that they themselves feel 'sissy'. They need to feel that their masculinity is appreciated and that they can be different and separate from you without always being competitive. Any sexist behaviour should meet with strong disapproval but empathy concerning their struggle to be accepted as 'one of the boys' should also always be shown. Finally, boys need to be encouraged to find their own way of being a 'New Man' and should never be expected to feel guilt about the 'sins' of other males. Steve Biddulph's book *Raising Boys* is a very helpful guide on this subject.

Fostering Social Awareness

This involves giving children a balanced and realistic view of the world, and encouraging discussion and thought on ways to solve or cope with the 'disasters' which consistently make headline news. Make sure that there are plenty of opportunities to experience the variety and spice of life! Support their vision for the future.

> My mother always made me feel, not so much by what she said, but often just by her attitudes, that there was nothing that was impossible, that whatever I set my eye on I could do, so she never blunted my vision.
>
> ARIANNA STASSINOPOULOS

Valuing and Encouraging the Father's Role

This point is last but certainly not least. The majority of mothers are still raising their children in partnership with a man, and I am writing at a time when one of the best-selling posters is that of a beautiful naked man fondly cradling a baby in his arms. I suppose it is good news that fatherhood now has sex appeal, but research still indicates that the New Man movement still has not brought nearly enough equality into the parenting partnerships. Make sure that you use all your assertive skills to ask 'Dad' to do much more than a token share of the childcare and other work involved in running the home and family. If you are not living with the father, this means ensuring that fair maintenance is fought for and access is encouraged.

When you think that your partner is not pulling his weight (perhaps in spite of his good intentions), don't slip into feelings of victimization and powerlessness or dose your partner with 'put-downs' of men: insist on a quiet rational discussion. It may be that you have both slipped into stereotypical habits. This can so easily happen when you relax into intimacy. Just check that you are not 'taking over' the main parenting role (perhaps encouraged by the children, who themselves are prey to media messages of ever-nurturing Mums). Many women do because it often feels 'easier to do it yourself than nag'. Needless to say, this is no way forward for the positive woman, who does not make a habit of opting for short-term 'peace' solutions to long-term complex problems!

When the going gets tough (as it inevitably will in these transitional times) remind yourself that you are not just negotiating and fighting for more time and space for yourself, but for an important *principle*. Shared parenting is fair and just. Also, through demonstrating the rewards of shared parenting by our example and personal contact with children, we are, hopefully, laying down the foundations of a more equitable society for future generations while, more certainly, impressing upon our children that justice is an unquestionable human right.

> Equal parenting would leave people of both genders with the positive capacities each has, but without the destructive extremes these currently tend towards.
>
> NANCY CHODOROW

Giving Children with Special Needs Special Attention

There is a widespread myth that one of the most important marks of a good parent is that they can and do treat *all* of the children of a family in exactly the same way. A nightmare which haunts so many caring and responsible mothers is to find themselves guilty of loving one child more than another. So the 'good mother' makes supreme efforts to divide her resources of time, attention and material goodies *equally* amongst her brood. She will pride herself on the fact that there are no special favours for any of the children – whether the child be a welcome firstborn or an unwanted afterthought, female or male, the prettiest or the ugliest, the genius or the dunce, the angel or the black sheep, the healthy or the disabled, the natural or the adopted.

My quarrel with this apparently laudable approach is that reality can rarely live up to the myth, and that trying to make it look as though it does can lead to phony, insincere behaviour which can be very confusing and damaging to children. Also, our personal need to feel and be the perfect parent can take priority over the real needs of our children.

Perhaps some women are blessed with an abundance of maternal love which is totally unconditional and undiscriminating – but I haven't met one yet! Most of us mortals find it easier to love some children more than others and if we face this uncomfortable truth we can very often correct the 'imbalances'. Seeing our children more as individuals and responding appropriately to their *differing* needs can foster closeness and love. There are very obvious and socially acceptable ways of doing this, such as playing tennis with the sporty ones and chess with the intellectuals, but I am thinking more of other kinds of needs. For example, a child who:

- is physically small or in ill-health may need more protection
- is introverted may need more quiet periods alone with a parent
- is extrovert may need to explore the world at an earlier age
- is an insecure step-child may need more tolerance over tantrums or teenage rebelliousness
- has been let down by their father may need more encouragement and opportunity to spend time with other adult males
- is a boy might need extra time to adjust to the birth of a baby sister
- is young may need less time and attention given to explaining problems in the family, such as a bereavement or divorce
- is disabled may need more treats, material resources and reassuring attention
- has very different interests and aptitudes from you may require more time to talk, explain and demonstrate their skills or may need more space to be separate from you
- is fostered or adopted may need very special attention when it comes to the 'birds and the bees' talks.

I am aware that I could fill several books with such examples. Parenting children according to their individual needs and not according to what we need to give them not only makes them feel special and loved but also makes them more capable of understanding and accepting the real world, where some people will always need more support, attention and resources than others.

Sometimes we are too close to our children to really be aware of their special needs. Fortunately, we live in an age where we can seek outside help. If one or all of our children, perhaps because of their family situation, health or personality, should require special attention, there is now an abundance of books, self-help groups, charitable and statutory organizations which can help us. The positive mother does not believe that there is virtue in soldiering along in ignorance; she is willing and able to seek help and overcome her fears about spoiling and favouring one child more than another.

Working Co-operatively with Parents and Other Parent Figures Outside the Family

The movement into the world of work by women and the break up of many nuclear families are just a couple of reasons why many children nowadays have more than just their natural parents as parent figures. Other figures may be step-parents, visiting Dads married to other 'Mums', childminders, nannies or grandmothers who at times feel more like 'Mum' than the real mother, and also teachers at school who make take an interest.

Having a variety of parental input can be enriching, but it can also be confusing to the children if their 'parents' are constantly at war with each other, and even be terrifying if they find themselves used as weapons or pawns in the adult conflict. Many of the problems that these kinds of special parenting relationships can bring up are complicated and too full of emotional turmoil to be satisfactorily dealt with in this book, but the following very general guidelines may be a good starting point. Use them as a checklist.

- Be very clear about your roles and boundaries. Make sure that you, the other adults concerned and the children know who is in absolute charge at any given time.
- Work hard at establishing a genuinely friendly relationship with the other parent figures or, if this is not possible, keep your contact business-like. This is easier for the children to handle than an awkward, false game of 'happy families'.
- Do not quarrel over 'rules' and parenting practices in front of the children. If you have differences, face them head-on and negotiate a way of compromising or coming to terms

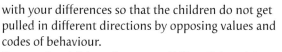

with your differences so that the children do not get pulled in different directions by opposing values and codes of behaviour.

- Do not give children the responsibility of choosing between parents and parent figures until they are mature enough to do so. (The British courts suggest that 12 years is the age when children's views about parental care should be taken into account – if you are unsure, ask for help from a counsellor and a specially trained family conciliator.)
- Give children *plenty* of time to adjust to any new parent figures who may come onto the scene, especially if they may be stepping into the shoes of a loved natural parent.

> 'Why does Daddy have to go away for such a long time? Unless there's some other woman he wants to marry! Thinking about that makes me sick ... I wonder who the woman is? I hate her already. I will never speak to her. Not as long as I live.'
> JUDY BLUME (in her children's novel *It's Not the End of the World*)

The difficulties of the step-parenting relationship, for example, are well known, whether it be through the fairy stories about wicked step-mothers, statistics in the press about violence from step-fathers or personal experience, but how often do we hear about the successes? If you look around, you'll see hundreds and hundreds of examples of families who have successfully worked through the inevitable web of jealousy and mistrust which seems so threatening in the early months of second marriages or early fostering relationships.

Here are some guidelines:

- Do encourage children to talk about their experience with other parents, but do not pry and resist making comparisons. If a child compares you to another parent, just point out that every family is different and don't forget to add that you understand how difficult and confusing it must be at times for them. Never allow children to play you off against each other – but don't be too shocked if they try!

- Watch out for, and curb, any competitive feelings you may have (e.g. 'If he can take them to France, I'll take them to Disneyland'; 'If she buys a new T-shirt, I'll buy a skirt.')
- Don't be afraid of open conflict – in fact, encourage negative feelings to be aired rather than buried.
- Resist becoming a peacemaker between your children and other parent figures such as absentee fathers, disapproving grandparents and despairing stepfathers. Encourage them to sort out their relationships, but keep well out of the middle!
- If a natural parent has gone missing, deserted the family or died, do talk about him or her – don't let the subject become taboo. However, only give information which you think can be appreciated and understood by the child and which is relevant. Try to be as objective as possible when giving the 'facts'. If you find yourself giving a subjective opinion, especially about their role as parents ('He's so irresponsible – wasn't fit to be a father'; 'She doesn't seem the maternal type ...'), remind the child that that is *your* opinion and you can understand that they may well feel differently about them.
- Encourage your children to talk to others who may have had similar experiences of divorce, bereavement or adoption. If you don't know anyone, look out for helpful books and magazine articles which will help the child feel that they are not alone in having conflicting, ambivalent, inexplicable feelings for the various parent figures in their lives.
- Keep a sense of perspective and remember that today's children are very adaptable and perhaps more open to the idea of multi-parenting than we might have been ourselves. Also remember that children's concerns often

My mother and father are both speaking to solicitors. I expect they are fighting over who gets custody of me. I will be a tug-of-war child, and my picture will be in the newspapers. I hope my spots clear before then.

SUE TOWNSEND *(The Secret Diary of Adrian Mole Aged 13¾)*

differ from our own – for example, the state of a teenager's complexion sometimes *feels* just as, if not more, important than conflict between the parents in their lives!

Friends and Relations

Firstly, perhaps, I should explain what I mean by 'relations' – I am thinking about anyone, other than your partner or children, with whom you are related by blood or law. Secondly, you may wonder why I have grouped them together with friends. I have done this because for most people nowadays their roles are interchangeable and indistinguishable. In western society the extended family is no longer the powerful force it used to be. It used to be people's main form of social and practical support, and set the values and rules which the individuals belonging to it lived by. Nowadays, friendship groups centring around work or a leisure pursuit can be equally forceful in both these respects. A girl friend may feel and act more like a sister than the blood relation you only see at Christmas and the boss at work can be more like an aunt than that comparative stranger who hardly remembers your name.

Only very rarely does anyone *initially* come to me for help over problems to do with these relationships, but once people begin to look closely and critically at their lives, difficulties in these areas tend to loom well into the foreground. Previously such relationships may have been 'taken for granted' or just not seemed as important as issues at work or more intimate relationships at home. But I have noticed that once people start to become more self-confident and positive in their feelings and actions, these relationships change, often very dramatically. Some relationships are enriched and nurtured because their value has been highlighted; others become more 'low-key' or are ended because they are now seen to be insignificant or damaging. The latter are often replaced by new relationships arising naturally from the increased social opportunities which a more positive lifestyle almost inevitably brings.

EXERCISE: NEGATIVE ASPECTS OF MY FRIENDSHIPS

*Use the following questions as triggers to set you thinking. Don't
bother with the ones which are not relevant to you. You may also
sometimes want to replace 'friend' with 'relation' and vice versa.*

Do you ever feel
- *bored when you are out with a friend*
- *irritated when you are at family gatherings*
- *the odd one out in your circle*
- *resentful about being compared to other relatives*
- *that you can never be yourself with your relations*
- *that you hold back on your 'success stories' for fear of making
  your friends jealous*
- *that your male friends always seem to want more than just a
  platonic relationship*
- *that you give more than you get*
- *that you are in competition with your friends*
- *that your confidence and trust is abused*
- *that you are a subject for gossip behind your back*
- *that you are going through the motions of duty with relatives*
- *that you do most of the compromising with friends*
- *that our friends are for fair weather and fun and are not really
  'there for you' when you are miserable*
- *the black sheep of the clan.*

*Make a list of problems you have in relating to various people
and note whether a problem occurs all the time or only on certain
occasions or in certain company. For example: 'I feel intimidated
by Charlotte when I am in a group with her' or 'I always seem to
fall out with my sister at Christmas and I end up giving in to her'
or 'I am never able to keep up platonic friendships with men.'*

After doing this exercise, the life of a hermit may have certain
attractions – but of course these relationships can be very
rewarding and worthwhile and often are the mainstay of our
lives. Partners may come and go and children move on to
pastures new, while friends and other relations can remain

steadfastly constant. They can give us invaluable feelings of kinship and community and provide a sense of continuity in a fast-changing and alienating world. Also, they can give emotional and practical support in times of difficulty and can share in our fun and joy in the good times.

> In a time when 'networking' and 'power' meals are the preferred means to meet people who presumably can help advance one's career, I long for the fine, out-of-fashion notion of 'best friend' ... A best friend can get you through the ups and downs the way no one or nothing else can.
>
> NANCY AUSTIN

So before giving up on your existing relationships, let's consider some of the factors which may be preventing you from having the kind of relationships with friends and relatives which you may need and want.

● Your 'auto-pilot' may be feeding you with messages which are either out-of-date or not relevant to your kind of relationships and so you become confused and cynical. You may have been given the impression that:

- Blood is thicker than water (but that's not your experience).
- Charity begins at home (so why are you the poor relation?)
- It's an ill bird that fouls his own nest (that's why it's always your fault).
- A friend in need is a friend indeed (no wonder it's difficult to trust).
- Friendship: the older it grows the stronger it gets (that's why you can't say good-bye or allow the relationship to drift apart even though you're bored and irritated).
- Don't wash your dirty linen in public (that's why you keep your pain and disappointment locked away and never ask for objective help).

● Your self-esteem may be too rocky.
- You may be trying too hard to please everyone for fear that no-one will want to be with the real you. So, in

order to avoid rejection, you may hang on to your moans and grievances, causing the relationship to stagnate or deteriorate.

- You may be expecting too much.
  - Perhaps you want your friends and relations to fulfil all your needs. In reality, often we can only get support from some and fun or a sense of community from others. A macho uncle or office colleague will not be able to give the same kind of support as your soul-mate from your women's group.
- You may not be assertive enough.
  - You may not be able to give and take compliments to feed the relationship or give and take criticism to refresh it. You may not be able to ask directly for what you want, or you may have stored up irritation and anger which, if let out, could have brought you closer.

> No one can make you feel inferior without your consent.
> ELEANOR ROOSEVELT

- You may be full of negative feelings.
  - Maybe you are suffering from envy, jealousy and resentment because your life isn't as happy and successful as you would want it to be. And you may be *expecting* to have a miserable time with your friends or relations.

> I have lost friends, some by death ... others by sheer inability to cross the street.
> VIRGINIA WOOLF

- You may not be giving enough time or effort to the relationships.
  - You may be spreading your sociability and caring too thinly, or relying on luck or other people such as your partner to provide the friends and not taking enough trouble to select your own.

If any of the above is ringing those unwelcome bells again, make a decision to revitalize your friendship network. Here are some ideas:

1. Decide what kind of relationships you need. Do you want emotional support, practical help, a sense of community ...?
2. Decide what you are prepared to put into the relationships, how much time and effort.
3. Decide what initiatives you need to take – renegotiating 'contracts', cutting down on time given to some relationships, ending others, and so on.

Don't forget, either, that you need support through the good times, pats on the back and genuine compliments when you are doing well. In our culture these are not as forthcoming as they could be, so be assertive and ask for them!

MAKING NEW FRIENDS

> So much of woman's relating revolves around supporting one another through the difficult times. But, when a woman seems to be doing well, support may be less forthcoming and she may feel as though she is cast out of the company of women.
>
> LUISE EICHENBAUM and
> SUSIE ORBACH

Perhaps this exercise has revealed just how shaky your friendship network has become. But making new friends sometimes requires a positive determined effort. To begin with we need to find ways of putting ourselves in situations where we will meet more people and then we need the social skills and confidence to use these opportunities to change relationships from a superficial to an intimate level.

Increasing Opportunities

When we are children and young adults opportunities to meet and make new friends are plentiful. A few adults then move on to work in environments where they meet a wide range of people, but the majority of us often find ourselves very restricted by the nature of our work or the pressure on our time. Many people I see find they do not even notice their lack of friends until they reach a crisis and find they have no one with whom to share their pain. This is one of the main reasons why I run so many groups, because it gives my clients an opportunity to build close supportive relationships. These group courses almost always result in the formation of a close, lasting friendship network of people from all walks of life and of all ages.

But of course, attending personal development groups is obviously not the only answer! You can join any number of activity-based groups such as adult education classes, social and sports clubs, political parties, pressure groups or business and professional women's associations. Your local library will have a catalogue of all the clubs and societies in the area. Almost all will agree to people coming along to one meeting before join- ing, so you can do the rounds before making a commitment.

Alternatively, you can use your holiday time to meet new friends by choosing a venue or organization which specializes in bringing people together. The travel industry has just woken up to the fact that many people's need to make friends is greater than their need to lie in the sun for a fortnight, and so there are an increasing number of options coming on to the market. Gone are the days when there was a stigma attached to a woman 'resorting' to going on holiday alone. People are choos- ing to go on their own because they know that they have more chance of making new friends than if they are 'stuck' in the company of someone with whom they were having a holiday just for the convenience of having a 'ready-made' companion.

Developing the Skills and Confidence

The first thing to remember is that you do not have to be the world's greatest extrovert to meet people or make new friends! Many people I know feel they can't make friends because they hate big groups and large social gatherings such as parties. They have often tried to find friends by braving these occa- sions and have only ended up feeling even more lonely. So unless you really are an extrovert in embryo, look around for quieter locations in which to practise your friendship-making skills. Here is a 'programme' you might like to try:

- Start by taking the opportunity to strike up conversations with people whom you are unlikely to meet again, in a place where there is a defined time limit to your meeting. (You might use supermarket queues or bus journeys.) The advantage of having a definite limit to the conversation is that you won't have the added worry of wondering how to get out of it when you dry up or it gets 'too hot to handle'.

- Move on then to doing the same in situations where you are more likely to meet the other person again, such as collecting the children from school or popping into the local shop. Disclose information about yourself that will give away your interests and values – if the other person is also looking for a friend this will give them opportunity to 'take the bait' and disclose something about themselves. If they do not want to extend the relationship they will probably just make polite noises and then you know that you would be better off moving on to other opportunities!

  If the exchange has gone well for you, end it before you get too anxious by taking the initiative to close the conversation, saying that you enjoyed talking and hope that you'll meet again. If they reciprocate, you could suggest making a more definite arrangement. Don't rely on the vagaries of luck to give you the opportunity of meeting again!

  The art is to throw out leads which the other person then has the choice to follow or not. Once you have started consciously practising this social skill yourself, you will begin to notice when other people do the same with you and you can then choose whether or not to have a bite at their bait. Remember that making friends is a legitimate social game and one that can, and should, be fun. If it feels more like fencing within the confines of a torture chamber, change your location without delay!

- Go on then to build up the friendship on a mutually assertive basis, always being direct about your needs and wants and encouraging the other person to do the same. For example, don't make excuses to ring up when you need to chat – say clearly why you are ringing and ask if it is a convenient time. If it isn't, ask when would be a good time to ring. As the friendship progresses, help to maintain it by occasionally starting up a discussion about your relationship by saying what you are getting out of it and asking your friend whether they are getting what they need and want from you. If you are not used to having this kind of conversation with friends, this may sound a very 'formal' way of operating to you at first but remind yourself that you are feeling this is only because it is new behaviour – not because it is forbidden! Even if it is a little embarrassing, a small amount of temporary discomfort might be a small price to pay for having the kind of friendship which is mutually satisfying.

> Many a friendship is lost through lack of speaking.
>
> ARISTOTLE

The positive woman ensures that she has the relationships that she deserves.

CHAPTER 11

Give Your Lifestyle a Management Boost

It's hard to remain in a positive mood when you:

- are totally disorganized
- find yourself always in a hurry
- are always late
- burden yourself with too many commitments
- are never able to find anything
- never have time to sit and discuss important matters
- feel torn in different directions
- have too many thoughts buzzing around in your head
- find your credit card unexpectedly over its limit
- learn that the telephone is about to be cut off.

Management skills should not be the exclusive prerogative of high-powered business executives; we all need them and can use them at home as well as at work. You certainly will appreciate them if you are doing the juggling trick of running a home, family and job!

Imagine that you are a highly paid management consultant brought in as a troubleshooter to your life – given that you are not allowed to fire yourself, where would you start? My guess is that you would probably recommend a time management course!

Time Management

> Gain time, gain life.
>
> PROVERB

How often do you hear your-self say 'If only I had the time ...' or 'That's all very well for those who have time to spare ...'? Perhaps you have been saying something similar as you have been reading this text so liberally scattered with exercises and action plans! But you probably know people who always seem to 'make time' to do the things they want to do – and don't you envy them? I am constantly hearing people saying 'Where do you find the time to do all that' – hoping maybe that there is some secret supply hidden under a bed!

Time management can not only give you extra hours to fill with activities of your choosing but also extra energy – because the time when you are in action isn't spent so stressfully.

EXERCISE: TIME WASTING

Use the following questions as a checklist, and then note down any other ways in which you waste time.

1. **Do you have clear goals and objectives?** *Knowing what you want and having a clear idea about the boundaries of your various roles helps you to prioritize. So often we spend inordinate amounts of time on trivial or non-urgent tasks, simply because we lack clear direction.*
2. **Do you think ahead enough?** *Or do you muddle along, flitting from one thing to another, hoping to get through it all?*
3. **Do you respond rather than initiate?** *Are others more in control of your time than you are?*

4. ***Do you use your 'good' and 'bad' times*** to their full advantage, or do you end up doing the most important things when you are tired, pre-menstrual or likely to be distracted?

5. ***Do you say 'no' often enough*** or do you still try to please all of the people all of the time? Do you take too much pride in your 'open door' or 'open arms' image?

6. ***Do you delegate enough*** or do you hold on to too many jobs which others could perhaps do just as well, if not more efficiently?

7. ***Do you waste time by being too tired or too tense*** and not working as efficiently and creatively as you could otherwise?

8. ***Are you too obsessional?*** Do you feel that once you have started something you have to always 'see it through' or make it perfect? Are you too 'house-proud', perhaps wasting your most creative hours ritualistically completing mundane chores before you can 'get down to something'?

9. ***Are you too untidy?*** Cluttered desks may not be quite a sign of a cluttered mind but they do not promote efficiency, while having a dishevelled appearance doesn't help you to feel effective unless you're in a business where that image is the uniform.

10. ***Are you too miserly?*** Do you waste hours hunting for the cheapest items or spend days doing tasks it would make better economic sense for others to do? Are you reluctant to take taxis or trains, which could give you extra hours in which to work or just allow you to sit and think?

11. ***Are you a slave to the telephone?*** Do you feel compelled to answer it or keeping chatting for longer than is necessary? Do you make calls when sometimes it would be quicker to write a short note?

12. ***Are you over-polite?*** Do you waste hours making small talk with people you don't want to talk to? Do you overload your speech and writing with laborious over-justifications and polite messages when directness and brevity would suffice? Do you make visits to people who don't really appreciate your 'kindness', or do you feel compelled to invite people back just because they have hosted you? Do you feel you always have to return a favour, however willingly it was given?

> 13. **Do you take full advantage of technology?** *Or do you pride yourself in liking the old-fashioned way? Do you refuse to believe that 'bought' cakes are edible? Do you think that the Internet is beyond your comprehension ...?*

I would guess that there are very few of us who wouldn't be guilty of some of the above – just writing this exercise reminded me of so many of my own bad habits which I often allow myself to slip back into. Some of you may work for organizations who continually check your time management, but those of us who are answerable to ourselves will also benefit from regular appraisals and new resolutions. If you have a serious problem, book yourself onto a time management course or at the very least buy a book which will give you a more detailed programme to follow. In the meantime, the following list of 'time savers' might be useful.

TIME SAVERS

1. **Time costing.** Put an economic value on your time. You may need to cost your skilled time differently from your time spent on more mundane or less lucrative activities (e.g. preparation, travelling, childcare and housework). Becoming freelance has made me confront the economic value of my time and enabled me to break very many time-wasting habits. Aim for a balance between the lucrative and less lucrative hours – that balance will need to be a personal decision based on your values, needs and goals.

2. **Spring cleaning** – without waiting for the right season! Regularly sorting out the muddle of accumulated clutter will enable you to check that everything you need can be quickly accessed. Doing something very practical like this also helps to get us into 'efficiency mode' and feel more 'centred'.

3. **Management equipment.** Even if you are lucky enough to have a secretary to do this for you, take yourself to a

large office supplier and look at the wide range of equipment designed for efficiency. This ranges from sticky reminder notes and filofaxes to computers. Buy some for home use as well as the office, or alternatively take the ideas and create your own cheaper version.

4. **Time allocation.** Study your energy levels and reallocate your time so that you are using your most creative hours on the most difficult tasks. Keep 'spade work' for the time when you usually coast along. Keep similar tasks together – for example, set one time for letters and other times for phone calls or reading. Set aside one day only for shopping. Make it clear to others around you when your 'Don't disturb' hours are to be.

5. **Delegate.** Women are reputed to find this more difficult than men. Your time costing might have opened your eyes to the hours you spend doing tasks which could be done more cheaply or more efficiently by someone else. Alternatively, you could train someone else, either at home or at work, to do some of your tasks, so that you could, perhaps, move on to doing something more challenging.

6. **Regular breaks.** Taking time off before you get too tired to relax will save hours by making sure that you use your energy most efficiently. (See the section on pressure management, pp. 112–13.) Also, having a break just to ponder a while will improve your creativity and enable you to come up with solutions to problems more quickly.

Home Management

This is obviously a vitally important area for women as we have been conditioned to think of the home as being our base and the special territory where we can prove our worth! Television advertisements continue to reinforce these messages: research has revealed that women are still twice as likely as men to be shown doing cleaning and washing. The reality is just as unfair, with research indicating that even when women work full time they still do very much more housework than men. Taking a more managerial attitude to the running of the home can help correct this discrepancy, which often simply results from habit taking over from reason.

PRACTICAL STEPS

> Life's too short to stuff a mushroom.
> SHIRLEY CONRAN

The following are some of the main areas where you may be able to initiate change and beat the Superwoman/Earth Mother/Cinderella myths which inhabit our subconscious and feed us negative feelings of guilt and inadequacy.

Time Management

Almost all the general points made in the last section can apply to your role in the home. Do a TM study for you and any family you may have. Negotiate a list of rules and start a rota. Include children as early as you can, but make their tasks interesting and progressively more challenging – don't just fob them off with setting the table three times a day! A few hours initially spent on training others to cook, mend, iron and shop will add months, if not years, to your life's supply of time. A few pounds a week on payments for the dishwasher, the window cleaner or fast food deliveries will similarly give you valuable hours to spend on lucrative work or recuperative leisure.

Assertiveness

This will help you to persist in imposing your list of rules and help you save time by not getting into arguments which lead nowhere. You will have more energy to put into creative tasks in the home because you are not worn out by an unfair share of 'spade work' and a build up of energy-consuming resentment.

Team-building

See your family or partnership as you would a working team: give yourselves plenty of time to meet together to discuss your 'working' relationships, air grievances and negotiate house-work rotas – as well as giving each other positive feedback and news. Many families rely too much on communicating with each other through third parties. There must be time for direct communication between all family members. Such meetings don't have to have formal agendas and minutes – you could do your 'family business' over a meal together. It is also helpful to have a regular daily slot for some 'family time'. In my case, because we all tend to work and play rather irregular hours, this is 9.30 or 10 p.m., when we all sit down for a snack together. If there is resistance to meeting together like this on a regular basis, insist on at least one gathering to check that there isn't something wrong with your relationships and com-munication with each other. Don't wait for a crisis to bring you all together, because that is not the best time to sort out 'everyday' issues of home management.

If you find you can't talk easily to each other even though you may want to, find a counsellor or family therapist who may be able to help you understand what is going wrong. Just a few sessions with an outsider can often help dispel blocks to communication and feeling (although, of course, they cannot produce love where none exists).

Nest-building

Assuming that family relationships are OK, just walking through our own front door should give us a warm positive glow because we become surrounded by an environment that feels 'at home' with us and our lifestyle. Check that your living space is meeting your needs, even though this may mean deviating from current fashion trends or having to 'face the music' from a bossy or over-cautious partner. Do you want your home to have a peaceful relaxing air or do you want it to be lively and stimulating? Perhaps different rooms could meet varying needs and moods.

If you live with others, do you have enough privacy? Have you at the very least a little corner which feels as though it is your personal space? In very many families the children have their own bedrooms, the husband has his office and/or his workroom – and the wife has nowhere special.

Does your home feel safe and secure enough? Have you, for example, become involved in a neighbourhood watch scheme? Does your home feel part of a community? Do you spend time getting to know your neighbours so that you can support each other? Now that so many women go out to work, shopping is done in impersonal supermarkets and children are minded or schooled some distance from home, friendships amongst neighbours do not just 'happen' as they seem to in the 'soaps', so we have to make a conscious effort to befriend each other.

Planning

Of course home should be a place of spontaneity. Maybe there could be more of that if some families didn't spend so much time coping with crises! Do you look ahead enough? For example, what kind of maintenance will the home need next year? Who will look after whom if illness or even death should occur? Have you made wills? Have you checked out potential guardians for any children you may have? This may sound morbid, but it is highly practical, and remember that the positive woman is a contingency planner. Does every member of the family take responsibility for noting (preferably on a central note pad) that you are running low on baked beans or toilet paper or that the washing machine is making a funny noise? Does every adult member of the family add their major 'engagements' such as holidays, parents evenings, business dinners, etc. to the family diary – and take responsibility for organizing any necessary baby, dog or granny sitting that needs to be done? Does it all sit in the lap of the gods? Or is it left up to you?!

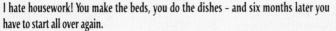

> I hate housework! You make the beds, you do the dishes - and six months later you have to start all over again.
>
> JOAN RIVERS

EXERCISE: HOME MANAGEMENT

Make a list of all the improvements you think you could make in this area of your life, discuss them with anyone else affected by them, such as your family, and then set some goals.

For example:
1. *Family meeting to discuss rota for housework – 2 August.*
2. *Buy home diary/planner – tomorrow.*
3. *Central heating service contract – by Friday.*
4. *See solicitor re wills – make appointment.*

Financial Management

I cannot pretend that this is my strong area. I have already admitted that, in spite of my maths qualification, I can now barely count my change and certainly don't remember my tables. But I have learned, like many other women who have been through a divorce, to keep as tight a control of my own finances as I possibly can – even if this means spending extra money for accountants to do my sums.

Men still dominate not only the personal financial worlds of most families but also the financial power bases in both the public and private institutions of our society. Many women are taking great pains to change this state of affairs, either by becoming more

> My situation was like a lot of women's. I didn't know exactly what my husband's income was and never bothered to find out because we had a very comfortable lifestyle ... women are too damned nice.
>
> ANN SMITH (Investment Consultant) describing her struggle to get a fair divorce settlement

knowledgeable and skilled themselves or by campaigning for changes in educational policies and attitudes which steer girls away from these areas. Perhaps you are one of these. If not, you could:

- Ensure that you are knowledgeable about basic budgeting and book-keeping practices and use this knowledge to keep control of your own and any joint financial venture you may be involved in.
- Ask to go on an appropriate training course if your job involves preparing budgets or any other financial task.
- Fund yourself to go on a course if you plan to climb the career ladder or run your own business. Many of the women's management organizations run seminars and training days. Take as much advice as you can from other sources of help such as your bank or the Small Business Advisory service.
- Start using financial jargon (once you have learned what it means!) This will communicate that you understand 'asset turnovers', 'price earning ratios', 'profit growth indexes', 'shareholder's equity', etc.
- Check out for yourself your insurance and pension rights. Be present at meetings with bank managers, insurance executives, etc., when any joint policies are discussed, and understand your financial position should your partner die or the marriage break down. Very many women don't even know where the appropriate papers are kept.

> Money is better than poverty, if only
> for financial reasons.
> WOODY ALLEN

Work

> Nothing can convince me that people are at one with their work unless they are joyous about it.
>
> INDIRA GANDHI

Does the very word 'work' send shivers down your spine or make your brow furrow or your eyes brighten? Your reaction will depend partly on your personal state and also the nature of the work in which you are involved.

> In order that people may be happy in their work these three things are needed; they must be fit for it, they must not do too much of it, and they must have a sense of success in it.
>
> JOHN RUSKIN

If the quote opposite is true then maybe it is no wonder that for years women have suffered more depression than men! Women's work has for centuries been low status and reputedly 'never done'. Moreover, repeated childbearing hardly kept our forebears in peak condition. Career-building was an option that was only open to a very tiny majority of privileged women and most of these were unmarried.

The central focus of this chapter will be largely on paid work which could, or does, form the basis of a career – although much of what I will discuss in this section may be relevant to women who work as 'housewives', mothers or volunteers for various organizations. Women are only just beginning to see for themselves the attraction that a career has had for men. It has the potential to be not only a source of 'bread', but an important source of self-respect and happiness.

YOUR CAREER

Do you feel that your job is giving you, or has the potential to give you, these hidden benefits, as well as being an adequate source of income? Many women do not. Although there is reputedly equal opportunity to take advantage of these benefits, the reality is that women are still losing out compared to men.

In general, the picture seems to be that although sex discrimination laws have changed 'appearances' and helped enable women to get into the job market, it is still very hard work for them to get the same satisfaction and success as men.

I acknowledge that there are many complicated reasons for this state of affairs and many of these need to be tackled in the economic and political arenas, but I have witnessed many individual women taking very significant steps forward by addressing their personal issues and taking a positive strategic approach to making changes.

> The oldest habit in the world for resisting change is to complain that unless the remedy can be universally applied, it should not be applied at all. But you must begin somewhere.
> WINSTON CHURCHILL

The following section is designed to help you check out your needs and wants in your working life and look at ways in which you can take action.

EXERCISE: MY WORK OBJECTIVES AND PATTERNS

1. In searching for my ideal job I would consider ...

Tick the appropriate box

	v.important	important	unimportant
job satisfaction	☐	☐	☐
potential for power	☐	☐	☐
job status	☐	☐	☐
opportunity for challenge	☐	☐	☐
career development potential	☐	☐	☐
high salary and fringe benefits	☐	☐	☐
security	☐	☐	☐
opportunity for teamwork/ colleague support	☐	☐	☐
social contacts	☐	☐	☐
flexible working hours	☐	☐	☐

childcare facilities and
   arrangements   ☐   ☐   ☐
proximity to home   ☐   ☐   ☐
work and company is
   ethically sound   ☐   ☐   ☐
....   ☐   ☐   ☐
....   ☐   ☐   ☐
....   ☐   ☐   ☐

2. In the past the following factors (or any others) have
   influenced my choice of work:
   – money
   – location
   – luck
   – nepotism.

3. My immediate priorities are ...
   – to find a job with more money
   – to find more work satisfaction
   – to consolidate my present position.

Once you are sure of what you want and what you have to give to
the world of work, the next step is to find a way of 'making it
happen'!

WAYS FORWARD

I realized that I was not a soldier, or a philosopher or a politician; I could cure no disease, solve no economic problems, or lead any revolutions. But, I could dance. I could sing. I could make people laugh. I could make people cry.

SHIRLEY MACLAINE

Whatever women do they must do twice as well as men to be thought half as good. Luckily this is not difficult.

CHARLOTTE WHITTON

Boost Your Motivation

It is so easy to get set in a working rut. Sometimes this is a rut that we chose, or was chosen for us, in early schooldays when firstly opportunities for women were much more limited and secondly, our knowledge of ourselves and the world was severely restricted.

Read
Magazines and newspapers now often include stories of women who have made a success of their working life. Make a point of reading these and collect the ones which interest you. Many articles are additionally interesting because they illustrate how people have coped with specific blocks to progress such as discrimination, sexual harassment, physical handicap and, of course, inadequate childcare arrangements.

There is also an increasing supply of books on the market written specifically for women who are wanting to make changes in their work, and a few of these are included in my booklist. Ask your librarian or bookseller for details of more.

Go Networking
Find ways of meeting other women who take a serious interest in their work. You can do this by attending courses or joining relevant groups and organizations. Many of these are led by women who are successful in their work and they can become very inspiring role models. Often the subject matter of the discussions and lectures is of direct interest. 'Motivation', 'Are you Making the Most of your Skills?' and 'Where can I go to Next?' are topics typically found in the calendar of events.

Start to 'Look the Part'

Thank goodness we have progressed from the days when women had to pretend to look like men in order to make any headway in the world of work. Some of our pioneering ancestors such as Dr James Miranda Barry (1795–1865) had to spend their entire careers in male disguise (Dr Barry even felt obliged to bear her child in secret). But we do still have to acknowledge that male values and prejudices still exert influence in the masculine atmosphere of most women's working worlds.

I'm not suggesting that you too must adopt a dark suit to be taken seriously (although some women in the more traditional professions still swear that they need to do so). But it is important, at least in the early stages of your career, to be respectful of the current clothing 'tradition' in your place of work. Be willing to compromise. Spend time closely observing how other women are dressed, especially those on the rung of the ladder just above you. At your interview and for your first few years, this may mean dressing a little more boringly or conventionally than suits your personality. But be reassured that the way fashion trends are now going in the world of work, when you reach the boardroom you will be able to be as flamboyantly feminine and creatively eye-catching as you want to be.

MAKE YOUR PRESENT JOB MORE SATISFYING

It may make a good deal of sense to concentrate some energy into your present position before moving on – if indeed that is what you do want to do. Doing this could not only make your working life more rewarding, but also boost your self-esteem and improve your chances of getting a good reference. No-one can tell you how hard your particular boat can be rocked – you will have to find that out by experimenting with gentle rolls which won't initially threaten your paycheck and prospects. The following exercise may help you to become more aware of how you could take some action.

EXERCISE: MY PRESENT JOB

Use the following questions as a checklist and stimulus to new ideas.

1. *How can I improve my own performance – with a view to making the best out of my present situation?*
   Could I:
   - *improve my time management and delegate more*
   - *become more assertive*
   - *ask for more responsibility*
   - *prepare myself for meetings and speak up*
   - *check out training courses and ask for secondment*
   - *go on stress management course?*
2. *In what ways could our work as a team be improved?*
   Could we:
   - *hold regular staff meetings (at Monday 8.30 a.m. so that everyone is present)*
   - *have more social time together (perhaps convert the back room into a place to have coffee and read journals, etc.)*
   - *suggest a discrimination awareness workshop*
   - *press for more secretarial help*
   - *argue the case for an outside facilitator to run the next training session*
   - *suggest inviting a speaker to explain the latest legislation in order at least to start people thinking and talking?*
3. *What extra resources do I/we need to campaign for?*
   For example:
   - *an up-to-date computer with servicing contract*
   - *some assistants*
   - *a new telephone system*

> But the fruit that will fall without shaking
> Indeed is too mellow for me.
> MARY WORTLEY MONTAGUE

LOOKING FOR A NEW JOB

Nowadays it is not good enough to sit around waiting for that golden opportunity to turn up. Of course 'lucky breaks' do play their part in the careers of successful people but rarely are they as significant as ambition, determination and shrewd planning. Even if we are fortunate enough to meet an unexpected opportunity, we are much more likely to make good use of it if our 'job-hunting mode' is fully operational. The following suggestions may help you to enter that mode.

Use Advisory Services

I am always amazed how few people seem to be aware of these and think that walk-in Job Centres and newspapers are the only ways to find out about opportunities. Here are some ways in which you can make use of the services on offer:

- ask to see someone for free advice at the Job Centre – they may also offer you a computer analysis of your aptitudes and be able to match these with potential vacancies or retraining possibilities
- check your local directories for the names of private agencies and consultants
- approach professional organizations and unions who will usually send you literature and put you in contact with someone in your area to advise you about general recruitment policies and the level of local vacancies
- ring or write to personnel departments of large organizations of interest to you – they may give you tips on where the 'holes' in that particular job market are likely to be found.
- use your personal grapevine – although you may not want everyone at work to know what you are doing, perhaps there are trusted friends or family members who may know someone who can advise you or put you in contact with someone who knows someone!
- create your own website.

Prepare Your Curriculum Vitae/Résumé

This is a summary of details about yourself, a résumé of your skills and background. If you haven't seen one, there are often specimens to be found in books or through one of the above agencies. The general consensus is that it should cover a maximum of two sheets of paper. Always get someone else to read it over who knows you well, because it is likely that you will have undersold yourself, as selling oneself seems so akin to boasting, and that is difficult to do in most cultures.

Never lie on your CV or application forms, but rather practise presenting 'negative' information in a positive way. For example:

- a period of unemployment can be described as 'an interesting period which gave me time to seriously reflect and seek out new opportunities and experiences'
- a long spell of sickness is 'an experience which taught me an invaluable lesson about keeping fit and helps motivate me to keep my body in its present good state of health'
- a disability has 'given me a sensitivity to others in difficulty and an acute awareness of the value of taking a positive approach to problems.'

> Transform failure into success!
> JOHN ROCKEFELLER

Always have your CV printed on good quality plain paper and have several copies readily available. Update it on a regular basis – if you have access to a computer this is very simple and quick to do, and you can keep your original on disc.

Try Speculative Applications

Send your CV together with an individually written covering letter to firms and organizations where you would like to work. It helps if you follow this approach up with a telephone call. If you are not sure to whom to send the CV, ring first to make sure that it does land on the most appropriate desk. Many employers are impressed by this assertive approach, especially if it saves them advertising and agency fees!

Prepare Well for Interviews

This is always a good idea – even if the employer gave the impression that this will be a 'very informal affair'. Here are a few ideas worth noting:

- Summarize main points you want to get across on small cards which can easily fit into a pocket or handbag. These might include your strengths, skills, weaknesses (reframed in a positive way) and questions. Although ideally it is better to memorize the information on the cards, I have known people to bring out the cards in the actual interview. If you are going to do this, explain assertively what you are doing rather than try to take the odd sly glance at your notes. If you are stuck for an answer, you could say (as you produce your cards), 'It is interesting that you should ask that question, as I was just considering that issue last night and made some notes of the major relevant points.' A quick glance at your headings should be enough to get you back on track again and is a preferable alternative to drying up or waffling. Many interviewers will be impressed by such assertive behaviour and pleased to see that you have given the interview very serious consideration.
- Read as much as you can about the organization and if possible talk to people who are already employed there. Then make sure in the interview you let it be known that you have taken the trouble to do this 'homework', perhaps by asking a quesion on some information that you picked up in your research. Also find out about competitors, if relevant to do so.
- Prepare answers both to obvious questions and to questions which you are afraid might be asked. These may include sexist questions (about your marital status or

children, for example) which, in spite of the law, are still
frequently used. If you are prepared you will be less likely
to get inappropriately uptight and defensive. Have positive
counter-arguments to hand – how your experience of
being a parent could have advantages, for example – and
assertively assure the interviewer that you have considered
all the practical difficulties and have strategies to cope
with them. Rarely is an interview the right time or place to
fight the feminist cause!

● Use role-play with friends to practise dealing with tricky
interviews or overcome phobic attitudes. Many people
simply don't apply for new jobs because they can't cope
with the interviews! But this problem can be overcome, as
my work in Assertiveness Training has proved over and
over again. Assertiveness Training may be particularly
useful to you and your self-esteem if you are returning
to the job scene after many years of being at home with
children, or have had a long enforced period of
unemployment.

Consider Setting Up in Business on Your Own

> If you want to do something, you find a way. If you don't want to do anything, you find an excuse.
>
> ARAB PROVERB

Setting up in business is
becoming an increasingly popular option for women. There
are many reasons why they
choose to take the risk of
becoming their own boss.
Many do not feel that they fit
into the masculine world of the established businesses and
large corporations; others choose this option because it seems
the only way of being able to satisfactorily combine the role of
career woman and mother, and some just want an outlet for
their creativity and sense of adventure and a chance to 'do
their own thing'. Unlike most entrepreneurial men, very
few women actually start off believing that this is the way to
make big money – in fact quite the opposite, as many (like
myself!) make a conscious decision to opt for less money

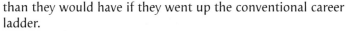

than they would have if they went up the conventional career ladder.

If you do decide to think seriously about starting your own business, there are many advisory services, books and courses now available to help you, but the first step is to decide whether you have the personality suited to this way of life. This is probably even more important than having any special ability.

EXERCISE: AM I A POTENTIAL ENTREPRENEUR?

Answer the following questions.

1. Am I a leader?
2. Do I make decisions quickly and easily?
3. Do I enjoy competition?
4. Do I have self-discipline and will-power?
5. Am I a planner?
6. Do I enjoy making contact with new people?
7. Do I like working hard?
8. Am I prepared to work many and/or unsocial hours?
9. Do I look after my body well enough to stand the physical strain?
10. Am I emotionally resilient enough to be able to stand the stress?
11. Am I the kind of person who is excited by risk-taking?
12. Am I the kind of person who doesn't mind dropping my standard of living if necessary?
13. Am I the kind of person who allows myself to make mistakes?
14. Am I flexible enough to be able to play many different roles?
15. Am I prepared to do many hours of uninteresting 'spade work' if necessary?
16. Am I prepared to be on my own for long periods if necessary?
17. Can I say 'no' easily?
18. Could I fire someone or make anyone redundant if necessary?

19. *Am I a reasonable judge of character?*
20. *Do I believe I have the right to be successful?*

If you said 'yes' 20 times – ask yourself what is holding you back?!

If people knew how hard I worked to acquire this talent, they would no longer be surprised.

MICHELANGELO

There's no such thing as bad times. I kept telling myself. There's no such thing as bad business. Business is there if you go after it.

ESTÉE LAUDER

Leisure

I am interested to observe that I planned this as the last subject of this section. Perhaps I am more inculcated with the 'woman's work is never done' myth than I like to believe! I have to admit that I do have strong 'workaholic' tendencies. My excuse is that I enjoy my work, even though I also very much enjoy 'playing' or just idling away hours in a totally purposeless fashion. But even when I know that my relaxation hours are well earned, I still have a tendency to fill them up with 'useful' tasks or make my 'play' into a chore by setting myself unrealistic challenges. Fortunately, most of the time I have the upper hand over my workaholic habits and have managed to 'waste away' whole weeks at a time without feeling guilty!

I know that I am not alone in my difficulty in giving leisure adequate space in my life. It is a very common problem in our modern competitive culture with its emphasis on 'speed' in so many of the ordinary everyday activities we find ourselves doing. For example, how many of us spend our week-ends just pottering around the house or wandering casually around the market doing more chatting than buying? Perhaps we are trying too hard to keep up with 'Superwoman' who greets even Saturday with a five-minute aerobic energizer and quick bracing shower followed by a three-minute breakfast on 'instant vitality' cereal or pre-sliced bread popped into the high-tech toaster beside the fast-boil kettle and then a dash to the supermarket to 'beat the crowds'. There she can 'whizz round', picking up the pre-cut, pre-scrubbed, pre-packaged goodies for her busy self and family. On her way home, she may grab a bracing coffee in the 'Quick-Bite' cafe so that she can have a hasty flip through the brochures she picked up when she nipped in to the travel agent's next door. But her dreams of jetting away to leisurely days in far-away primitive lands are soon terminated by the pressing reality of having to rush to the garden centre sale so that she can spend Sunday giving her backyard its instant spring look!

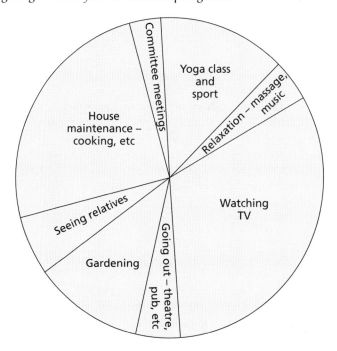

My leisure hours

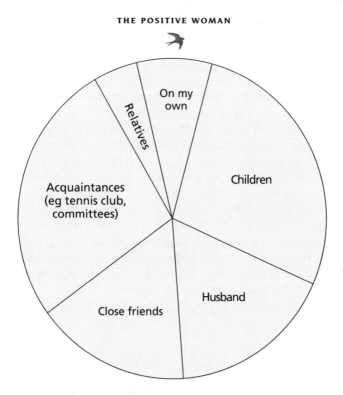

The people with whom I spend my leisure time

Are your leisure hours equally frantic? If they are, are they 'frantic' in the way you want them to be, or could you manage them more effectively so that you can get the fun and relaxation you deserve? Completing the following exercise should help you gain a better perspective.

EXERCISE: MY LEISURE

1. How many leisure hours do I have, on average, per week?
2. Draw a pie chart to indicate how these are spent.
3. Draw another chart to indicate the people with whom you spend your time.

4. *Taking two coloured pens, shade in your pie charts with different colours to indicate how much of your time is spent on activities which you enjoy and how much is spent on activities which you actually dislike. Leave blank any others.*

5. *Note down some reasons why you may not be getting the leisure time you want and deserve. For example:*
   - *I don't plan ahead well enough.*
   - *We spend too much time trying to do everything together.*
   - *I don't save.*
   - *I can't say 'no' to friends I don't want to be with.*
   - *I work too much.*
   - *I'm too house-proud.*
   - *I'm an over-conscientious mother/daughter.*
   - *I worry about what others will think.*
   - *I've just got in a rut and need new ideas.*

6. *Note down some of the actions you can take to change the above and take more control. For example:*
   - *join a save-as-you-earn scheme for holidays*
   - *encourage the children to do activities on their own or in a club*
   - *go to the library every week to collect 'what's on' leaflets and look through the new book section.*

7. *Set an immediate goal for yourself to do something different this week-end. Tell someone what you intend to do and ask them to check up on you on Monday morning!*

Remember, all work and no play makes Jack a dull boy – and it doesn't do much for Jill either!

The positive woman constantly monitors the balance in her life.

FOUR

Practical

Support

CHAPTER 12

Positive
Action
Strategy

I know from my own bitter experience that reading a book like this can sometimes leave you feeling overwhelmed. Perhaps at the start you feel very inspired and enthusiastic, but feelings of despair and apathy can seep in as you turn each additional page and find yet another problem with which you identify, or yet another suggestion you could take up. In true *positive* fighting spirit, I have therefore devised a strategy to help you regain your motivation and prepare for action!

This strategy will help you to focus on four important areas which, in my experience, are often not given careful enough consideration and it will also help you to identify the action you will need to take in order to make sure that your good intentions take their place in the real world. Once again I have used a mnemonic sentence to help you remember each section.

| GOOD | STRATEGIES | REAP | SUCCESS |
| GOALS | SABOTAGE | RESOURCES | SUPPORT |

Goals

I have stressed several times in this book how important it is to learn to set yourself *realistic* and achievable goals. Negative thinkers habitually set themselves up for failure by choosing goals which are inappropriate. We have already noted how if we do not have enough self-awareness or self-knowledge, we can set ourselves up for failure by aiming too high, too low, or simply not in the direction best suited to our aptitudes and skills. In addition, we have seen how an inability to think creatively or use effective decision-making skills can seriously limit our options.

Once we have set realistic goals, it is important also to check out our unconscious selves for any hidden motivation. Many people feel an apparently inexplicable sense of disappointment when they reach their targets. One obvious reason may be they miss the 'high' which the adrenalin-producing challenge stimulated, but another may be that, in addition to their openly declared goal, they often had a 'hidden motive' which was not satisfied, and indeed may never be able to be satisfied.

A useful way of checking out your unconscious wishes is to ask yourself what do you actually *want* as an outcome from your action and secondly, what can you *reasonably expect*. More often than not there will be a big difference between the two because our 'wants' originate from needs of the Child or Parent parts of our personality and the 'reasonable expectations' are the considered judgements of the Adult part of us (see pp. 35–6 for a basic explanation of this theory). Quite often our 'wants' are kept a secret even from ourselves simply because they do feel 'childish' and unreasonable and are not perhaps very socially acceptable.

Consider these examples:

Identified goal: To find a new and more satisfying job

Hidden motivation: To make the company realize what an invaluable job I am doing – so when I am offered a new job I find myself making excuses not to 'paint the town red' in celebration because I was secretly hoping colleagues would be devastated by my news.

Identified goal: To join the Parent/Teacher Association to improve the standard of my daughter's education

Hidden motivation: To make new friends – so I find myself supporting all the social events and not saying anything challenging or divisive in the meetings.

Identified goal: To improve my relationship with my husband

Hidden motivation: To find someone who will give my husband a 'good dressing down' – so I find myself getting irritated by the marriage guidance counsellor's impartiality and reluctant to attend the sessions.

If you confront any unconscious motivation you may be harbouring, you can keep better control of it. So you are more likely to be able to maintain a cool rational perspective on your goals and to appreciate your success.

In considering your goals, it is also helpful to distinguish between your short and long-term aims. Try to identify at least one step towards your goal which you can take in the very near future, so that you can feel a sense of achievement early on in your 'campaign'.

Sabotage

In this section you will need to look at some of your negative habits. How are you likely to prevent yourself from achieving your goal? If you have worked through many of the exercises in this book, you should already have a good idea of how you habitually stop yourself from getting what you want and deserve. For example, you may:

- put others' needs before your own too often
- not prepare yourself well enough
- demand perfection from yourself and others
- not be prepared to persist
- be unwilling to risk being disliked
- be a prisoner of your fear of loneliness.

Also, you will need to consider 'outside' factors which may sabotage your chances of success, either directly or indirectly. These may be to do with other people's apathy or antipathy or the environment in which you are operating. Consider whether the atmosphere surrounding your 'campaign' is conducive to it, or so alien and unsupportive that you may be better taking your precious energy elsewhere.

Resources

The first task here is to assess the resources you already have to hand in order to help you tackle the problem. Examine your own relevant personal qualities, knowledge and skills. This can be a very empowering exercise, as we rarely put enough value on our 'strengths' when faced with a problem – we tend to think first and foremost of the resources we lack.

Secondly, it is a good idea to review other avenues of help which may be available to you through friends, work, charities, the bank, etc.

Finally, note what action you will need to take in order to secure the resources which you lack.

Support

There are no extra prizes for soldiering through your 'campaign' without help and encouragement! So don't make the task of dealing with your problem more difficult and lonely than it need be. Remember that negative-thinking people tend to surround themselves with friends and colleagues with similar attitudes. So you may need to look outside your immediate circle of 'friends' to find people who will give you the encouragement and support which you need. Don't forget that you may need to go to different people for different kinds of support. Some people will be useful because their arms are ever open for a consoling hug, others are more able and willing to give encouraging constructive advice and criticism.

You may need to take some practical steps towards getting the kind of support which you need. Try:

- telling your friends to remind you of your 'reasonable expectation' and to warn you when you seem to be going off track
- arranging formal or informal meetings and/or 'supervision' sessions with a colleague, counsellor or solicitor.

Listed below are three examples of how to apply this strategy to specific problems.

POSITIVE ACTION STRATEGY – EXAMPLE 1

Problem: I Need a More Stimulating and Satisfying Job

Goals	Sabotage
Short-term: Clarify the kind of job I want	*Myself:* I get too tired to think
Assess the market	My fear of being rejected
Long-term: Get a job with more responsibility	*Others:* John's cautiousness
	Competition for the job

Action: Prepare new CV
Get career counselling
Buy papers

Action: Early nights
Confidence course/book
Temporary loan

Resources
Own: Seven years' work
    experience
Part-time university course
Good with people
Efficient organizer
Computer literate

Support
Gill; Angela

Other: Books
Role-plays with friends
Good references

Other: University tutor
Career counsellor

Action: Ring referees
Practise interview skills

Action: Talk to Frank and
    Angela
Meal out after every interview

POSITIVE ACTION STRATEGY – EXAMPLE 2

Problem: Darren's Poor School Report

Goals
Short-term: To get more
    information from the school
To find out whether Darren
    is really happy

Sabotage
Myself: My prejudice against
    teachers
My high expectations
My ignorance of curriculum,
    time-table, etc.

Long-term: To get a better
    report next term
Possibly to change schools

Others: His Dad's impatience
Influence of friends

Action: Ring school for
    appointment

Action: Share my worries and
    fears with Darren's dad
    (George)

Resources
Own: My assertiveness
My love for Darren
My own school experiences
The school handbook and
  governors' report
Education Advisor
Private tuition or remedial
  class
Books; videos

Support
George
Mum
Other parents
The history teacher who
  likes Darren
Darren himself
The governors

Action: Check finances
Set time to work on
  Darren's homework

Action: Talk to George
Ring Mum
Join PTA

POSITIVE ACTION STRATEGY – EXAMPLE 3

Problem: Lack of Safe Playground Facilities in Our Area

Goals
Short-term: Find out whether
  our area is unusually
  deprived
Make people more aware

Sabotage
Myself: I give up too easily
I hate speaking in public
I may get too angry

Long-term: New playground
  built

Others: Cutbacks
Political apathy

Action: Ring local
  organizations

Action: Go to Assertiveness
  class

Resources
Own: I'm highly motivated
I will give time to this project
Secretarial skills

Support
Neighbours
Friends
The press
Our Member of Parliament

Others: Fund raising
School fields
Joan – posters

Action: Hold car boot sale to
start fund going for
campaign

Action: Ring local radio to
plug cause and car boot sale
Form committee

The positive woman is a woman of action!

CHAPTER 13

Relaxation, Meditation and Creative Visualization

Relaxation

Twenty minutes of deep relaxation can be more refreshing than several hours of sleep, especially if you are over-stressed and your mind continues to work overtime in the production of lively dreams and nightmares. Relaxation is a basic requirement for maintaining positive thought and action. It can revitalize you physically, emotionally and intellectually.

When you are fully relaxed there should be a decrease in your heart rate and your breathing should be slow and regular. If you maintain this state for a while and remain completely conscious, you will experience a slight 'out-of-body' sensation as your brain waves actually change their pattern and bring tranquillity to your mind as well as your body. If you cannot recall having ever felt this kind of sensation you may need to spend some months doing daily exercises in order to train your body and mind in the art of relaxation. Once you have acquired the skill, you will find that you can switch yourself into this deeply relaxed, 'floaty' state for a quick five-minute 'pick-me-up' even in the most stressful of situations.

Today there are innumerable courses, books and tapes available, and you may have to hunt around for the method of relaxation which suits you best. The following are examples of very simple ones which I have found useful.

PROGRESSIVE RELAXATION

- Sit in a comfortable position with both feet fully supported on the ground, or lie on a bed or the floor.
- Check that your hands are loosely held on your lap or lying by your side.
- Close your eyes and take note of all the external noises around you.
- Become aware of your breathing and begin to make it slower and more regular by counting 'Breathe in, one, two, three; breathe out, one, two, three.' Continue this for a few minutes and then let yourself breathe easily and naturally.
- Beginning with the feet and gradually working upwards through your body, focus on each individual muscle in turn. Concentrate on checking that each feels heavy and relaxed. If it feels tense, clench it hard and then slowly release it. Repeat several times. Finish with stretching and contorting your face and allowing it to relax completely.
- Become aware of your breathing again and let your body become fully supported by the chair, floor or bed. Notice how heavy it feels and how light your spirit feels. Picture yourself floating away to an idyllic peaceful location of your choosing. Using your imagination, listen to the sounds of that place. Each time you find your mind wandering, bring it back to focus once again on the scene. (I often use a favourite spot in the Yorkshire Dales – I am lying on the banks of a rippling brook, under the gently rustling leaves of a beautiful old tree watching the magnificent clouds furl and unfurl. I use poetic licence to add some Mediterranean warmth!)
- When 10 to 20 minutes have passed, bring yourself back into the real world slowly by gently stretching and taking a couple of deep breaths.

You could make a tape to help you go through this exercise. Record your instructions to yourself, using the first person and the present tense:

> I am now becoming aware of my breathing ... my feet are now fully relaxed ... my head feels heavy and my mind light ... I can hear the rustle of the leaves ... I can feel the warmth of the sun ...

'QUICK FIX' RELAXATION

- Find a corner where you can't be seen. Roll your neck gently back and forth a couple of times and then shake your wrists, shoulders and ankles vigorously. Screw your face up tightly and then open your mouth and eyes as wide as you can several times.
- Close your eyes and take two or three regular deep breaths and focus your mind on your relaxing scene or mantra for a couple of minutes.
- Drop your shoulders and return to the fray!

Meditation

MANTRA MEDITATION

In the section on stimulating creativity, I have already described one method of meditation, using a mandala (page 53), but if this idea does not appeal to you, or you do not have a mandala picture to hand, try focusing your mind by using a word or phrase.

- Sit or lie in a position where your body can feel relaxed and comfortable, but not one in which you are likely to start dozing. Serious meditators often choose to sit cross-legged on the floor but an office chair or a seat in the bus can be used just as effectively once you have mastered the skill of temporarily detaching yourself from the outside world.

- Concentrate for a few minutes on your breathing, becoming very aware of its rhythm. Try to make this as regular as possible by counting.
- After a few moments on each breath, begin to repeat a certain word or phrase. It doesn't seem to matter what you use as long as it seems to work for you. Many people choose a word such as 'relax' or a phrase such as 'I am at peace with the world', but the technique could work just as well with 'sausages' or 'Puddles are wet.' This word or phrase then becomes your 'mantra' which you train your mind to recognize as the signal for meditation. Whenever your thoughts begin to wander, concentrate your mind back again on your mantra. Continue to repeat it for 5 to 20 minutes.

DANCE MEDITATION

This is a good exercise if you are feeling physically very tense and find that you cannot sit still.

- Prepare a small room or corner of your room by clearing it of furniture or piling up cushions against any hard or protruding surfaces.
- Select some rhythmic music which hasn't any particular emotional or thought-provoking content for you.
- Blindfold yourself and dance as vigorously as your 'padded room' will allow you. Whenever a thought begins to enter your head bring your mind back to concentrating on allowing your body to express the rhythm of the music.
- After 10 to 15 minutes, remaining blindfolded, lie flat on the floor and just concentrate on your breathing, allowing your body to become heavy and relaxed. By this time it should be quite easy to let your mind just 'float' for another 5 minutes.

COLOUR MEDITATION

This is a variation which I find very easy and soothing.

- Use any of the above methods to first get yourself into a relaxed state and then, on each 'in' breath, imagine that from the tip of your toes you are drawing in a kind of coloured 'earth energy'.
- Imagine this colour slowly and gradually seeping into your whole body and being released on the 'out' breath as a different colour (for example drawing in orange and breathing out white). Continue for at least 5 minutes.

Creative Visualization

This is a technique with which some alternative healers claim to be able to cure or halt even serious malignant diseases such as cancer. Many people have reported success from using their imagination to visualize their diseases and pain, and to melt them away with images or colours. I certainly cannot vouch for the use of creative visualization in the field of physical health, but I have found it useful in my work in helping people to improve their self-image and alter their behaviour.

USING PICTURES

One example of its use is to picture yourself in your mind's eye doing whatever it is that you want to do. Use your imagination to visualize yourself being successful, happy, confident, outgoing, assertive, angry or whatever it is you wish to be.

- Use one of the above relaxation exercises to get yourself into a deeply relaxed state.
- With your eyes closed, imagine the scene with which you are having difficulty looking as you would like it to look. Feel as you would like to feel. Then take yourself through

the scene or situation saying what you would like to say and doing what you would like to do.

- Repeat this exercise daily for a week or so before trying it out in the 'real world'.

USING IMAGERY

Another example is to use imagery to help you to banish persistent negative thoughts.

- Give your negative thoughts a symbolic form such as black clouds, wicked pixies, vicious snakes.
- Lie or sit in your relaxed state and imagine yourself gaining control of these thoughts in some imaginative and fanciful way. (You could return the pixies to the garden shed, lock its door and bury the key, or sweep the clouds away with a giant multi-coloured feather duster.)
- Replace these images in your imagination with symbols of positive thought, such as a beautiful object, a serene face or a galloping horse.
- Repeat this visualization often, until you are able to use it 'to order' in your everyday life to help you change from a negative to a positive tack.

Affirmations

Affirmations are positive statements which you say to yourself (usually out loud) while you are in a relaxed and receptive state of mind. Many people find them a very helpful way of starting the day. They are usually 'I' statements and are said in the present tense. My personal preference is that they should remain 'realistic'. That is because I know that I cannot 'con' myself with idealistic affirmations such as 'I achieve anything I want' or 'I write fluently and effortlessly' or 'I love everyone.'

I also feel that it is important not to bombard yourself with too many affirmations. It may be more helpful to limit yourself to only three or four phrases which you can easily recall and quickly repeat over and over again. For example:

'I am a unique person with untold limits of unique potential.'
'I am looking forward to getting to know and like more people today.'

Alternatively, you could use images and metaphors as affirmations. For example:

'I am a bird flying freely in the sky and I can land wherever I choose.'
'I am a lion, proud and protective.'
'I am a maturing oak, now solidly earthed to the ground but still gently growing and becoming more beautiful and interesting each day.'

Experiment with various affirmations until you find the ones that seem to give you the boost you need. Don't forget to repeat them often, preferably at a regular time while you are in a relaxed state.

The positive woman can relax whenever she chooses to do so.

CHAPTER 14

Asserting
Yourself

I have found that very often people do not stand up for themselves and what they believe in, not because they lack the skill to do so but quite simply because they do not feel that they *should*. Often if they give themselves time to think about their options rationally, they do believe that they have as much right as anyone else to have their needs, wants, opinions and endeavours respected, but their actions are so often dictated by the subconscious, where old messages, fears and anxieties are buried.

Assertive Rights

The following list of rights can help you to override this kind of negative conditioning. Read it over and over again – out loud to a friend if possible. If necessary, cover your walls with the list until you have well and truly locked it into your subconscious!

MY ASSERTIVE RIGHTS

1. I have the right to ask for what I want (realizing that the other person has the right to say 'no').
2. I have the right to have an opinion, feelings and emotions and to express them appropriately.
3. I have the right to make statements which have no logical basis and which I do not have to justify.
4. I have the right to make my own decisions and cope with the consequences.
5. I have the right to choose whether or not to get involved with the problems of someone else.
6. I have the right not to know about something or to understand.
7. I have the right to make mistakes.
8. I have the right to be successful.
9. I have the right to change my mind.
10. I have the right to privacy.
11. I have the right to be alone and independent.
12. I have the right to be an assertive person.

If you have difficulty in understanding or accepting these rights, try reading my book *Assert Yourself*, which gives a much fuller explanation. Always remember that these rights are universal and therefore everyone else deserves this kind of justice as well!

Finally, there is just one more right to mention:

I have the right to be a positive woman.

I do hope this book will help you to assert this vital right. As I said at the start, I know from personal experience how much more fun and satisfying life can be when we both think and behave in a positive way.

Good luck!

Further

Reading

This list is, of course, by no means exhaustive, but it contains many books which are in my own personal library and have proved very helpful to people working on the kind of issues discussed in this book.

Assertiveness and Confidence

Arapaki, Maria, *Softpower* (Warner Books, USA, 1990)

Berman Fortgang, Laura, *Take Yourself to the Top* (Thorsons, 1999)

Bower, Sharon and Gordon, *Asserting Yourself* (Addison-Wesley, USA, 1976)

Brown Glaser, Connie and Steinberg Smalley, Barbara, *More Power to You* (Century, 1993)

Dickson, Anne, *A Woman in her Own Right* (Quartet Books, 1982)

Feensterheim, Herbert and Baer, Jean, *Don't Say Yes When You*

Want To Say No (Futura, 1975)

Fenn, Dr Christine, *The Energy Advantage* (Thorsons, 1997)

Grant, Wendy, *Dare* (Element, 1996)

Gray, John, *Get What You Want and Want What You Have* (Vermillion, 1999)

Lindenfield, Gael, *Assert Yourself* (Thorsons, 1987; revised edn 2000)

—, *Self Esteem* (Thorsons, 1996; revised edn 2000)

—, *Super Confidence* (Thorsons, 1989; revised edn 2000)

Roet, Dr Brian, *The Confidence to Be Yourself* (Piatkus, 1998)

Shone, Ronald, *Creative Visualization* (Thorsons, 1984)

Zimbardo, Philip, *Shyness* (Pan, 1981)

Inspiration and Motivation

Christie, Agatha, *An Autobiography* (Collins, 1977)

Craig, Mary, *Blessings* (Hodder and Stoughton)

Dowling, Colette, *The Cinderella Complex* (Pocket Books, 1981)

—, *Perfect Woman* (Fontana, 1989)

Eichenbaum, Luise and Orbach, Susie, *What Do Women Want?* (Fontana, 1984)

Forsythe, Elizabeth, *Living with Multiple Sclerosis* (Faber, 1979)

Goldman, Emma, *Living my Life* (Pluto, 1988)

Henriques, Nikki, *Inspirational Women* (Grapevine, 1988)

Lindenfield, Gael, *Self Motivation* (Thorsons, 1996; revised edn 2000), cassette available

Maclaine, Shirley, *You Can Get There From Here* (Bodley Head, 1975)

Masham, Sue, *The World Walks By* (Collins, 1986)

Murphy, Kate, *Firsts: The Livewire Book of Women Achievers* (The Women's Press, 1990)

Sheehy, Gail, *Pathfinders* (Bantam, 1981)

Stott, Mary, *Forgetting's No Excuse: An Autobiography* (Faber, 1973)

Management of Feelings

Bach, George and Goldberg, Herb, *Creative Aggression* (Anchor Books, 1983)
Friday, Nancy, *Jealousy* (Collins, 1986)
Jeffers, Susan, *Feel the Fear and Do it Anyway* (Arrow, 1987)
Klama, John, *Aggression* (Longman, 1988)
Lindenfield, Gael, *Emotional Confidence* (Thorsons, 1997; revised edn 2000)
—, *Managing Anger* (Thorsons, 1996; revised edn 2000)
Lindenfield, Gael and Vandenburg, Malcolm, *Positive Under Pressure* (Thorsons, 2000)
Parkes, Murray, *Bereavement: Studies of Grief in Adult Life* (Penguin, 1975)
Rowe, Dorothy, *Depression: The Way Out of Your Prison* (Fontana, 1983)
—, *Beyond Fear* (Fontana, 1987)

Management of Lifestyle

Cranwell-Ward, Jane, *Thriving on Stress* (Routledge, 1990)
Garrett, Sally, *Manage Your Time* (Fontana, 1985)
Proto, Louis, *Take Charge of Your Life* (Thorsons, 1988)

Personality Development, Childhood and Parenting

Bettelheim, Bruno, *A Good Enough Parent* (Thames and Hudson, 1987)
Brown, Judith, *I Only Want What is Best for You* (Cedar, 1986)
Chodorow, Nancy, *Reproduction of Mothering* (University of California Press)
Conran, Shirley, *Superwoman* (Penguin, 1990)
Harris, Thomas, *I'm OK, You're OK* (Pan, 1970)
Miller, Alice, *The Drama of Being a Child* (Virago, 1987)

James, Muriel and Jongeward, Dorothy, *Born to Win* (Addison-Wesley, USA, 1985)

Lindenfield, Gael, *Confident Children* (Thorsons, 1996; revised edn 2000)

Proto, Lois, *Who's Pulling Your Strings?* (Thorsons, 1989)

Rowe, Dorothy, *The Successful Self* (Fontana, 1988)

Satir, Virginia, *Peoplemaking* (Science and Behaviour Books, 1972)

Skynner, Robin and Cleese, John, *Families and How to Survive Them* (Methuen, 1983)

Relationships

Austin, Nancy, *The Assertive Woman* (Arlington Books, 1988)

Blume, Judy, *It's Not the End of the World* (Pan, 1988)

Drs Connell, Cowan and Kinder, Melvyn, *Women Men Love. Women Men Leave* (Sidgwick and Jackson, 1987)

Eichenbaum, Luise and Orbach, Susie, *Bittersweet: Love, Envy and Competition in Women's Friendships* (Arrow, 1988)

Emecheta, Buchi, *Head Above Water* (Fontana, 1986)

French, Marilyn, *Her Mother's Daughter* (Pan, 1987)

Friday, Nancy, *My Mother, Myself* (Fontana, 1977)

Fromm, Erich, *The Art of Loving* (Unwin, 1962)

Goldberg, Herb, *The Inner Male: Overcoming Blocks to Intimacy* (Signet, USA, 1987)

Kiley, Dan, *Living Together, Feeling Alone* (Cedar, 1991)

Goldhor Lerner, Harriet, *The Dance of Anger: A Woman's Guide to Changing the Patterns of Intimate Relationships* (Grapevine, 1990)

Metcalf, Andy and Humphries, Martin, *The Sexuality of Men* (Pluto, 1985)

Naifeh, Steven and White Smith, Gregory, *Why Can't Men Open Up?* (Warner Books, USA, 1984)

Norwood, Robin, *Women who Love Too Much* (Arrow, 1985)

—, *Letters from Women who Love Too Much* (Arrow, 1989)

Positive Thinking and Creativity

Arieti, Silvano, *Creativity* (Basic Books, USA, 1976)
Bono, Edward de, *Six Thinking Hats* (Penguin, 1985)
Buzan, Tony, *Make the Most of your Mind* (Pan, 1988)
Lindenfield, Gael, *Success from Setbacks* (Thorsons, 1999;
    revised edn 2000)
Norfolk, Donald, *Think Well and Feel Great* (Michael Joseph,
    1988)
Peiffer, Vera, *Positive Thinking* (Element Books, 1989)
Roger, John and McWilliams, Peter, *You Can't Afford the
    Luxury of a Negative Thought* (Thorsons, 1991)

Work

Alson, Anna, *Equal Opportunities* (Penguin, 1987)
Argyle, Michael, *The Psychology of Happiness* (Methuen, 1987)
Bayley, J., *How to Get a Job After 45* (Kogan Page, 1990)
Harris, Jean, *Everything You Need to Know for Success in
    Business: The Woman's Guide* (Grapevine, 1990)
Hopson, Barry and Scally, Mike, *Build Your Own Rainbow; A
    Workbook for Career and Life Management* (Leeds Lifeskills
    Associates, 1984)
Josefowitz, Natasha, *Paths to Power* (Columbus Books, 1980)
Lindenfield, Gael, *Managing Anger at Work,* cassette (Thorsons
    2000)
NEC and Lucas, *How to Work Effectively* (Thorsons, 1988)
Reed, A., *Returning to Work: A Practical Guide for Women*
    (Kogan Page, 1989)
Wallis, Margaret, *Job Hunting for Women* (Kogan Page, 1987)

Index

Thorsons
Directions for life